COMBAT LEGEND

F–15 EAGLE
AND
STRIKE EAGLE

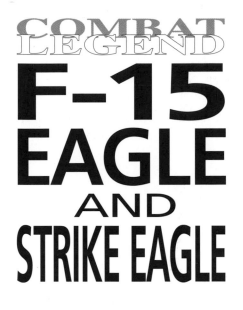

Steve Davies

Airlife

Acknowledgements

The author would like to thank the following for their help in producing this book:

SSgt Claudette Hutchinson, USAF; Capt. Randall 'Hacker' Haskin, USAF; Sqn Ldr Graeme Davis, RAF; Mike Smyth, Boeing; Garth Granrud, Boeing; Lt. Col Clarence 'Lucky' Anderegg, USAF ret.; SrA. Jason Passmore, USAF; Dennis R Jenkins; Lt. Col Gregory 'Yumper' Black, USAF ret.; Todd Blecher, Boeing; Major Joe 'Moca' DeFidi, USAF; Ted Carlson; Larry Merritt, Boeing

Special thanks go to: Paul F. Crickmore for his support and enthusiasm, Paul E. Eden for editing the manuscript, my parents for their help throughout, and to Caroline, who puts up with me.

Text written by Steve Davies
Profile illustrations drawn by Dave Windle
Cover painting by Jim Brown – The Art of Aviation Co. Ltd.

First published in the UK in 2002
by Airlife Publishing Ltd

British Library Cataloguing-in-Publication Data
A catalogue record for this book
is available from the British Library

ISBN 1 84037 377 6

Printed in Hong Kong

For a complete list of all Airlife titles please contact:
Airlife Publishing Ltd
101 Longden Road, Shrewsbury, SY3 9EB, England
E-mail: sales@airlifebooks.com
Website: www.airlifebooks.com

Contents

Eagle Timeline

26 June 1972
The first F-15A (71-0280) was rolled out in a ceremony in St Louis and christened 'Eagle'.

27 July 1972
The F-15A made its first flight from Edwards AFB, California, with test pilot Irving Burrows at the controls.

7 July 1973
First flight of the two-seat F-15B.

14 November 1974
F-15A/Bs entered operational service with the USAF's 555th TFTS at Luke AFB, Arizona.

1 February 1975
The Streak Eagle completed its sweep of all eight time-to-climb world records by streaking to an altitude of 30000 m (98,425 ft) in less than 3 minutes 30 seconds.

10 December 1976
The first F-15s were delivered to Israel.

26 February 1979
First flight of the F-15C.

19 June 1979
First flight of the two-seat F-15D.

27 June 1979
The first F-15 air combat took place during an IDF/AF mission over southern Lebanon. Five Syrian MiG-21 'Fishbeds' were shot down, for no losses.

15 July 1980
Japan accepted its first F-15J Eagle.

August 1981
The F-15 became operational with the RSAF.

20 June 1985
Rollout of the first MSIP F-15C.

May 1986
1,000th F-15 Eagle delivered.

11 December 1986
F-15E Strike Eagle flew for the first time, with McDonnell Douglas test pilot Gary Jennings at the controls.

12 April 1988
Delivery of production F-15Es began when the first F-15E arrived at Luke AFB for the 405th TTW.

November 1989
Last F-15C delivered.

12 September 1995
First F-15S delivered to the RSAF.

12 September 1997
First flight of the IDF/AF F-15I Ra'am.

2001
Boeing assembles the last USAF F-15E.

19 April 2001
South Korea orders 40 F-15Ks.

1. Prototypes and Development

Captain Jon Kelk, a 31-year old United States Air Force (USAF) F-15 pilot, had already spent a tedious four and a half months in the Saudi desert when he took to the air on 16 January 1991. Training sortie after training sortie had been flown; some right up to the Iraqi border to test the Iraqi defences and response times, some against low flying RAF Tornados to practise intercepting targets among the ground clutter which sometimes tricked his F-15's radar. This time though, he and his fellow squadron mates knew that it would be different. The order had been given – they were going to war. 'Of course, there was anxiety', Kelk later recalled, 'More than anything else there was fear of the unknown. I had little doubt that I was much better trained than my opponents, but even if your training is better, you never know if you are going to be fighting their best guy'. Kelk had reason to worry, US computers had predicted the loss of 150 allied aircraft on the first night of Operation *Desert Storm*.

Kelk walked to his jet and began the ritual of preparing it for tonight's mission, just like he had countless times before. Tonight though, his job as flight lead was to fly in the first wave of twenty F-15Cs arranged in a 'wall' formation. Their job was to take on any of the 500+ Iraqi fighters which might try to interfere with the waves of Coalition attack aircraft following only a few minutes behind. Some 80 km (50 miles) into Iraq, and three hours later, Kelk and his wingman (Rick Tollini) picked up an enemy contact on their radar screens. Kelk's radar warning receiver (RWR) lit up and a tone warbled in his earphones, indicating he was being targeted by this radar contact. 'I'm spiked', he radioed Tollini, as the contact climbed through 2134 m (7,000 ft) towards them. Despite electronic indications suggesting that the contact was a hostile fighter, Kelk held his fire – he could not be sure that this was so and was concerned that he might be targeting a friendly fighter whose identification friend or foe (IFF) equipment was malfunctioning.

As the two closed at over 2253 km/h (1,400 mph), Kelk had to make a decision, and fast. His RWR continued to show that he was being locked up, AWACS – the airborne warning and control systems aircraft with which he wanted to confirm the radar contact's status (friend or foe) was being hounded for similar requests by other fighters – he could not get a word in edgeways on the radio. With a final look at the radar contact's flight profile – climbing aggressively towards him – Kelk made the decision. He closed his eyes to protect his night vision, and pressed the pickle button on his control stick – the action needed to launch an AIM-7M Sparrow air-to-air missile (AAM). Simultaneously he wrenched his F-15C into a high-*g* turn while enthusiastically mashing a button on his throttle to command that his aircraft stream chaff behind it. Chaff is a bundle of aluminium strips which is released into the airflow to produce a false radar return. Kelk wanted it streaming behind him to confuse any missile which might already be in the air and headed straight towards him. In the race to get his aircraft adjacent to his enemy he failed to register

The F-4 Phantom was one of McAir's (McDonnell Douglas) best products during a time when several major defence contractors were producing fighters and bombers for the armed services of the United States of America. Despite the affection that its crews held for it, the 'Rhino' was by no means perfect; the air war in Vietnam would soon expose some of its weaknesses. (Boeing)

that he had not felt the AIM-7 leave his aircraft; there should have been a small judder and a rocket plume as the missile streaked away. He checked his armament control panel – it showed that he still had four of the missiles attached to his jet. With his mind racing for answers and his RWR still screaming at him in his headset, he thought, 'Oh, God. Now what do I do'.

In one of those moments where time 'slows down', Kelk was struggling to even sense a 'gut instinct'. His AIM-7, if it had fired, needed him to keep the target locked in order for it to guide; if the enemy had already launched his own missile then Kelk should manoeuvre even more aggressively and disregard the need to keep the target locked. He chose the best compromise that he could – he continued to pump out chaff while manoeuvring as aggressively as he could without losing his radar lock. Seconds later, as a pretty purple-orange 'sparkler' lit up the sky some 10 nm (18.5 km; 11.5 miles) distant, Kelk became the first American to score a kill in the F-15. Although Kelk did not know it at the time, his AIM-7 had launched, and guided, squarely into an Iraqi air force MiG-29 'Fulcrum' – Iraq's most modern fighter.

The F-15 had come of age. And so, the results of a 30-year programme had finally been combat-tested by the USAF. A programme

initially dubbed 'F-X', or 'Fighter Experimental', started when US Defense Secretary Robert McNamara gave the USAF funding to initiate a study to replace the McDonnell Douglas F-4 Phantom II on 7 January 1965. The result was the world's most feared and safest jet fighter. Almost 30 years later, F-X would boast an unblemished combat record of 100.5 enemy kills without a single loss.

Lessons learned

Forty years previously the Korean War had been waged. It had been a good conflict for US fighter pilots. The USAF's kill ratio had been 10:1, and the North American F-86 Sabre had achieved a highly respectable kill ratio of 7:1 against the much touted and more numerous Mikoyan-Gurevich MiG-15 'Fagot'. The MiG-15 was the latest Soviet fighter jet; designed to ward off imperialist fighters and bombers from the Russian homeland, it had been sold to North Korea for a similar reason. Many of the pilots flying the F-86 Sabre; a manoeuvrable second-generation jet fighter, had experienced combat before. They had flown North American P-51 Mustangs, Republic P-47 Thunderbolts and Lockheed P-38 Lightnings during World War Two, and were well versed in the art of air combat manoeuvring. They achieved their fine kill ratio because they could close in on a bandit, position for a guns kill and then accurately unleash a torrent of machine-gun fire into the enemy aircraft. However, following the battles in the skies over Korea, things soon began to change for the worse.

At the highest levels in the USAF and the Pentagon, a shift in tactical thinking was fast taking place. Project *Forecast*, a 1963 initiative designed to look ahead and evaluate the future of air warfare, had concluded that future fighter aircraft would fly high and fast. They would engage their foe with long-range missiles which could be launched while the enemy was still too far away to be seen by the human eye – a scenario which was later to be coined beyond visual range (BVR). Rapid advances in solid state electronics were allowing US defence contractors to develop missiles like the AIM-7 Sparrow; a medium-range (c.24–32 km/15–20 mile) semi-active radar homing (SARH) missile which could down an opponent BVR. The Sparrow would be guided to the target with a radar in the nose of the fighter, and, naturally, both the fighters and their radars were also becoming more advanced. In theory at least, one can see why the USAF saw this approach as being so attractive. The Soviets were apparently always at least a decade behind the US in their advancement of technology, and they lacked this BVR capability; their doctrine called for supremacy in numbers, not technological domination. US strategic bombers tasked with delivering their nuclear payloads over the Eastern Bloc region were able to fly higher and faster than any Soviet interceptor designed to kill them. In short, the top commanders in the Pentagon envisaged the key to future combat success in combat was being able to kill the enemy before he could kill you. In this case that meant using air-to-air missiles – dogfighting was to become a thing of the past…or so they thought.

No gun

In line with this vision, new US jet fighters were built and developed as missile platforms, not as dogfighters. The Convair F-102 Delta Dagger and F-106 Delta Dart featured massive delta wings which conferred great high altitude performance and made them well suited to very long-range, high-speed intercepts, but the delta wing was not advantageous in a dogfight scenario. The Republic F-105 Thunderchief and North American F-100 Super Sabre were attack aircraft whose main job was to fly into Eastern Europe with nuclear bombs. The F-105 in particular was made to do so at supersonic speeds. Neither was nimble nor manoeuvrable within the confines of a dogfight, although the F-105 could out-accelerate any adversary at low altitude. The later F-4 had a large wing, which became highly modified with devices to generate additional lift at slow speeds. Critically though, an internal gun was never installed as the additional weight was deemed unnecessary. The F-4 made its combat debut in Vietnam in 1965 and it soon became apparent that US crews in both the United States Navy (USN) and Air Force simply were not adequately equipped, empowered or trained, to counter the threat they faced. North Vietnamese MiG-17 'Frescos', MiG-19 'Farmers' and later MiG-21 'Fishbeds', operated under the control of Soviet advisers

who sat on the ground scanning the skies with radar – a system known as Ground Control Intercept (GCI). With a bird's-eye picture of unfolding events, these advisers kept the MiGs safely away from formations of US fighter bombers and their escorting fighters, until an advantage materialised and an attack could be made on their own, favourable terms. Sweeping in for slashing attacks at high speed, the MiGs would follow their controllers' vectors to the bombers, make a very high-speed single pass with cannon fire, and then disengage to fight another day.

For a variety of environmental and electronic reasons, the F-4's ARQ-72 radar often broke lock and its AIM-7 Sparrows would misfire or misguide. The AIM-9 Sidewinder was new and plagued by weaknesses: one pilot, Maj. William Kirk, said at the time, 'There I was, closing at a god-awful rate with Sidewinders in an overhead attack. I'm pointing those Sidewinders at the ground and they are just growling [an aural tone indicating a lock on] and sputtering like mad. Of course, all they are 'seeing' is the heat of the ground!' Missile dogfighting was simply not happening. In addition, crews were further irritated by the stifling directives issued to them by their leaders. The Whitehouse had imposed a set of inhibitive Rules Of Engagement (ROE) on

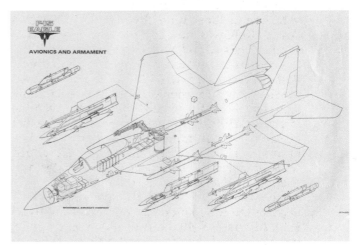

The F-15 was built around a weapons system which allowed for both air-to-air and air-to-ground weapons carriage. This early diagram clearly demonstrates that this time around McDonnell Douglas was going to build a gun into the aircraft from the word 'go'.(Boeing)

US air power, which governed what it could and could not do. Often, these rules drastically reduced the USAF and USN's ability to get the job done properly. As a consequence, crews became frustrated and disillusioned with their leadership, and MiGs continued to enjoy the protection of America's own ROE.

Once at the merge – the point where two fighters pass each other and make visual contact – the F-4 had lost much of its advantage. It could out accelerate the MiGs, but it could not out turn them. To make matters worse, US pilots had forgotten some of their dogfighting skills; they lacked the skill and knowledge to 'mix it up' with the MiGs, which were already fighting the battle on their own terms. US pilots had trained for years to counter the nuclear bomber threat and had spent more time practising long-range intercepts than they had dogfighting. Without a gun, it was next to impossible to do anything but disengage and reposition for a missile shot. Garth Granrud, a USAF veteran of almost 800 combat hours in Vietnam, and tours in the Cessna O-1 Bird Dog, Cessna O-2, Rockwell OV-10 Bronco, F-4D, F-102, F-106 and F-15, said

of the F-4's lack of an internal gun, 'Well, It must have been a mistake – we put it back in the E model, after all. The gun is a secondary, last ditch thing – I've used my missiles, I'm now defensive. Well, instead of running away, I can now knife fight with the gun. When we put the centreline gun [SUU-16A pod] on the D model it never aligned right, the dispersion was wide and the drag was horrendous. It was an afterthought at the time – the world was going to missiles and we didn't need the gun. I think we've rethought that one!'

It was the USN which took the initiative and assembled a cadre of laterally thinking fighter pilots to address the deficiencies in their dogfighting skills. The Fighter Weapons School was formed in 1969 to take the USN's best and most successful pilots and impart to them modern tactics and thinking. Almost instantly the effect was felt, as pilots flew back to the 'boat' (aircraft carrier) and passed on their newly acquired knowledge – in the month following completion of the first course, the USN shot down more MiGs than it had previously downed for the entire duration of the war. Eventually, the

Boyd's EM theory heavily influenced the design of the aircraft which was to eventually to emerge from the competition. This 23 February 1976 photograph displays the end product. Noteworthy is the simple design of the wings – distinctly lacking any high lift devices and straightforward in construction. This is F-15A-2-MC 71-0282. (Dennis R. Jenkins)

F-15A-2-MC 71-0283 pictured at Edwards AFB on 2 September 1973. The test airframes were initially painted in a gloss Gull Gray, and featured Conspicuity Orange wing and tail flashes. In the background can be seen the tail of F-15A 71-0282. (Mick Roth via Dennis R. Jenkins)

USN raised its own kill ratio from 3:1 in 1969 to 12:1 in 1975. Seeing their cousins in the Navy achieving greater success, the USAF also redefined such basics as formations, and introduced a more flexible approach towards modifying tactical gameplans while airborne. It too saw instant results. The overall kill ratio at the end of the Vietnam War was still just a dismal 2.5:1 however.

Granrud commented, 'It's a fair statement to say that the F-4 didn't do well in the air-to-air role. The F-4 was a great airplane from the standpoint that it did a lot of things ok; it didn't do anything really well though. It was a good bomber, and did get some good kills in SEA [South East Asia], but it was limited by armament, manoeuvrability and its weapons systems. I have fond memories of the F-4 – it was a big, tough airplane. In relation to the F-15, you had to be more careful in the way you flew it; it couldn't fly slowly and you couldn't horse around when that happened – it went out of control quite easily'. He added, ' There are other reasons that we didn't do as well as we could have – we were never really able to fight for total air superiority. If we had of done that we'd have knocked out every SAM [surface-to-air missile] site, every runway, and we'd have flown massive sorties to take care of the enemy's MiGs like we

did during *Desert Storm*. We were limited in some of the things we could do'. Granrud's allusion to ROE is understandable; the US Department of Defense (DoD) had placed heavy restrictions on when crews could engage MiGs.

F-X

At the same time as the US presence in Vietnam continued to grow, the USAF was commissioning its own study of both Soviet and US fighter jets. Headed up by Gen. John P. McConnell, who acted on reports made by Lt. Col John W. Bohn and Eugene M. Zuckert, Secretary of the Air Force, it concluded that Soviet interceptors posed a greater threat than had originally been envisaged. This, coupled with the relatively poor air-to-air performance in South East Asia and the allocation of $10 million for FY66 (Fiscal Year 1966) by Robert McNamara to design the ultimate US fighter, prompted McConnell to commission a study for a new fighter. The study would place greater emphasis on manoeuvrability than speed, would produce an aircraft costing between $1–2 million per airframe and having a production run of up to 1,000 airframes in total. The watch words for this project were to be 'air-to-air capability' – a focus played upon by McDonnell Douglas, whose F-X contender was later marketed under the slogan

'Not a pound for air-to-ground!', although those who held the purse strings (Congress) tried hard to force the USAF to concentrate equally on the air-to-ground mission.

Exercising the same sort of control as it had in the running of the Vietnam conflict, the American political system soon decreed that the F-X was to have an air-to-ground capability after all – it made better financial sense to build and buy a fighter that could perform more than just the one mission, the politicians said. USAF generals bowed to these demands with a wry smile however; it was a small price to pay for the opportunity to commission a dream fighter jet, especially one that they were not compelled to share with the US Navy. (At that time, Congress was heavily engaged in press ganging the USN and USAF into buying the same airframe designs, and here was an opportunity for the USAF to build a fighter to its own specifications).

A Request For Proposal (RFP) was sent to thirteen companies on 8 December 1965. With eight proposals received, the USAF selected Boeing and North American to take part in a four-month Concept Formulation Study (CFS). The CFS basically required the contractors to go away and come up with a range of designs to suit the USAF's needs. In October 1966, the USAF turned down all of the 500 designs that had been submitted. It was felt that none of them offered an airframe which would be optimised for the air-to-air role – all had made concessions to the air-to-ground mission which the USAF deemed excessive. Each company had opted to mount an internal cannon in their designs, a sign that lessons were indeed being learnt, but weight figures had ballooned to nearly 27215 kg (60,000 lb) – hardly an appropriate target weight for what was supposed to be a highly manoeuvrable fighter. Significantly, all of the designs had conformed to similar proposals offered for the USAF's TFX (Tactical Fighter Experimental) programme from a few years before (which resulted in the General Dynamics F-111 Aardvark). All had variable-geometry wings, twin engines mounted in their fuselages and all were heavy machines. Each made use of variable geometry wings (which could be swept back for high-speed flight and to a less-swept position for low-speed flight), a pair of high-bypass ratio turbofan engines, and shared avionics compatibility with the F-111.

In July 1967 the Soviets unveiled the MiG-25 'Foxbat', a very fast and high-flying interceptor designed to counter the North American B-70 Valkyrie. The Foxbat sent shockwaves through the upper echelons of the USAF. In a two-year period, the MiG-25 was to further shock the west by breaking a number of world speed records and time-to-altitude records. It was learned much later that the MiG-25 was far less capable than the Soviets had suggested and than US intelligence analysts had warned, but at the time it provided the final impetus needed to speed up the 'machine' which would ultimately produce the F-15. The unveiling of the 'Foxbat' paved the way for a second RFP on 11 August 1967. This went to the original eight contractors which had replied to the first RFP. This time it was clear that the F-X was to replace the F-4 Phantom.

Enter Major Boyd

The second RFP opened the door for unauthorised and unpopular work carried out by Maj. John R. Boyd to take centre stage in the future of aircraft design. Boyd, a test pilot and Korean War veteran who had been 'Chuck' Yeager's boss at 'Test Pilot School', had developed a new mathematical formula for defining the hypothetical performance and, hence, the design of modern fighter jets. It was called the 'energy-manoeuvrability theory'. This theory, published in May 1964, had been given little attention to date. It argued that a fighter's performance should be characterised by its potential and kinetic energies, each of which could be changed by manoeuvring the aircraft around the sky. It was this theory which would later mature into the 'Energy Manoeuvring' (EM) graph which fighter pilots now study to determine how much g they can pull and how fast they can turn their nose towards an opponent during combat. The EM graph allowed designers to take an aerodynamic shape and plot what energy state, lift, drag and other criteria would be placed upon it at a range of altitudes and airspeeds. Armed with this information, and using highly expensive mainframe computers, they were able to determine how well it would manoeuvre and, importantly, which portion of the flight envelope it would perform in best. The key advantage this system afforded was the ability to define tactics by studying a relatively straightforward graph and identify which flight regime offered the best performance advantages. How well one jet might perform against another could be assessed by comparing graphs for both aircraft. Thus, for the first time, aircraft designers could identify the weak spots of a potential adversary and design an aircraft which could exploit them.

Some three years after publishing it, the USAF accepted Boyd's theory. Criticism came from some quarters that Boyd had completed much of the work using mainframe computers without authorisation. Actually, he had devised the EM graph while assigned a desk job which had nothing to do with his 'extra curricular' study. The criticism came to nothing.

The second round of studies

Between the rejection of the first proposals in October 1966 and Boyd's theory being accepted, the USAF had revisited the Concept Formulation Stage. This was revised to produce a Concept Development Package and Technical Development Plan, and these were sent out in

August 1967. Yet, despite repeated attempts to have the air-to-ground portion of the mission removed from the Concept Formulation Package (CFP), the USAF was compelled to retain it, much to the dissatisfaction of those who felt that a compromise could never adequately be met. But Boyd's EM theory proved instrumental in the second round of proposals. It allowed the projected weight of the F-X to be reduced to 40,000 lb (18144 kg) from some 60,000 lb (29483 kg), although the designers were still hankering after a variable geometry wing similar to that of the F-111.

The CFP comprised four main areas for specific consideration: ensuring through wind tunnel tests that the aerodynamics worked; identifying suitable engines which would propel the F-X to

F-15A-1-MC 71-0281 seen refuelling from a Strategic Air Command KC-135 Stratotanker early on in the CDT&E trials. The F-15 proved to be a smooth, predictable and stable platform while taking on fuel, although problems with this phase of the flight tests were not expected. The refuelling receptacle in all F-15s is behind and to the left of the pilot. During refuelling, therefore, the pilot is unable to see the boom and must concentrate on staying in position with the tanker via a series of 'director lights' on the underside of the KC-135 or KC-10. (Boeing via Author)

its target top speed of Mach 2.5 and offer enough excess thrust to power the aircraft through combat manoeuvring; deciding on a good armament combination and avionics suite; and finally, deciding whether it should be crewed by one or two individuals. McDonnell Douglas and General Dynamics were both awarded contracts on 1 December 1967 to assist in refining the F-X project requirements. McDonnell Douglas had continued to develop its F-X design with company funding, despite not being selected after the first RFP. As such, its team was well placed to pick up the gauntlet even at this late stage. A supplement to the CFP was issued in August 1968 which effectively stated that the USAF no longer felt that the air-to-air mission would be all about shooting missiles from BVR. The supplement noted that smaller adversary platforms such as the MiG-15 should be small enough to avoid radar detection until a BVR encounter was too late. In addition, the final part of the second RFP, the Development Concept Paper (DCP) was issued around the same time.

Final round

In June 1968 the USAF took the results of the CFP and Technical Development Plan (TDP) for evaluation (which detailed the development schedule for the contenders' airframes). Several

The smaller speed brake of the first test F-15s had proved to create handling problems during its extension – buffet would vibrate the aircraft as the speed brake extended to an almost vertical position. McAir resolved the issue by enlarging the brake and limiting its range of travel. This is F-15A-1-MC 72-0280. (Dennis R. Jenkins)

factors caused considerable disagreement among the 100-or-so individuals assigned to the review board, but none more so than the avionics suite. The disagreement stemmed from whether or not the F-X should retain a terrain following radar (TFR) and bombing systems. These would allow the aircraft to bomb targets at low level, in bad weather, when they might not be visible to the pilot. Advocates argued that it should, especially given the fact that technology was advancing rapidly enough to allow the carriage of such systems with only a small weight penalty. Those against the idea argued that there were unacceptable risks in making such assumptions and that, in any case, these items were not essential and were costly overall. There were also strong voices among the ranks of experienced USAF fighter pilots, which reasoned that the F-X project was never going to succeed, and that a small 25,000-lb (11340-kg) fighter with simple avionics and super manoeuvrability was the way forward. Boyd was among this group. Many had witnessed the devastating effectiveness of North Vietnamese MiG-21s against the heavier and visually more discernible F-4. Indeed, some had taken part in secret USAF and USN projects on remote ranges in Nevada, where secretly acquired MiGs had been flight tested and evaluated against nearly every fighter in the US inventory (these programmes went under the codename *Have*. *Have Donut* was the name given to testing the MiG-15). In some respects, this band of dissidents was right to be sceptical of the success of what to some may have looked like just another F-4. Such was the weight of their argument that an airframe of the ilk they had aspired to develop was eventually built – as the General Dynamics F-16 Fighting Falcon.

USAF under pressure

With the review in full swing, the USAF came under pressure almost simultaneously from two external influences. The changing of president and the Navy's decision to ditch the TFX programme (F-111B), caused the USAF to cancel plans for a prototype testing phase of the programme. Instead, it chose to order the Full Scale Development (FSD) phase to begin. This rather underhanded scheme was also employed by the USN, which, having cancelled the F-111B, ordered the Grumman F-14 Tomcat into FSD

A close up of the early wing tip design adopted by McAir. The design was eventually changed to enhance the aerodynamics of the wing, although the formation strip lighting, navigation light and ALR-56 RWR antenna remained in place. This is F-15A-1-MC 71-0281.(Dennis R. Jenkins)

without seeing it through a prototype period first. The common driving force behind each service taking such a bold step was the change in presidency, due in November 1968. Each despised the idea of sharing anything with any other service: here was an opportunity to make the most of the confusion bound to result from a change in administration. By taking each project to the development cycle they could argue, with some justification, that they were too far down the road to cancel a project in favour of working with each other on a new, joint project.

The DCP – the last document to be issued before the June 1968 board convened to choose a winner – had defined that the aircraft was to be single-seat, capable of flying a 260-nm (482-km; 776-mile) mission on internal fuel; have excellent all-round pilot visibility; be twin-engined; and have a balanced combination of stand-off and close-in target-killing potential. In plain English, the USAF wanted a fighter with twin-engine survivability and good throttle response, which could out-gun and out-manoeuvre an enemy fighter in the event that it had not been shot down while still beyond visual range. Even at these later stages there was still an emphasis on the use of a swing-wing design. In addition, the USAF decreed that the engine, radar and other major components would be tendered for on a prototype basis – a move designed to attract the best systems at the least risk to the Air Force. The cost of each airframe had mounted, with 'turn key', or fly-away cost, being estimated at around $5.3 million each. The F-X airframe, once chosen, was to be designated as the F-15.

And the winner is...

With the F-X project guidelines decided upon, a final RFP was submitted to seven defence contractors on 30 September 1968. The last bids were received on 30 December that same year. Fairchild, McDonnell Douglas and North American each received $15.4 million to enter the Contract Definition Phase (CDP). The CDP called for a range of criteria to be fulfilled by 30 June 1969, the most notable of which were: a thrust-to-weight ratio approaching 1:1 at combat weight; a fatigue life of 4,000 flight hours; 360° view from the single-seat cockpit; and a gross weight of 40,000 lb (18145 kg).

On 23 December 1969, the contract was awarded to the McDonnell Douglas Corporation. Its Aircraft Company division (the famous McAir) was to prepare for an eventual production run of 749 airframes, provided of course, that McAir model 199-B could be produced within given financial guidelines – the USAF reserved the right to cancel the project if it went over 145 per cent of the target cost of $937 million. Of the 749 airframes, 20 would be used for testing.

After more than a year of solid testing in three wind tunnels, accumulating more than 22,000 hours of tests, McAir had finally come up with a very simple, fixed-geometry, cambered wing design, which featured smooth lines and a distinct absence of any high-lift devices. Such devices were a feature of the F-4's wing, but the F-15's wing had been designed to perform best at high subsonic speeds where dogfighting would typically take place – it offered a 21° per second turn rate, allowed greater instantaneous acceleration and provided a much slower landing speed of around 120 kt (222 km/h; 138 mph). Conversely, the F-4's wing had been designed to allow it to fly very fast with a minimal drag penalty, the down side to this was that it was not that efficient at the slower end of the speed spectrum, and therefore needed high lift devices to maintain adequate control and lift when landing and taking off.

It had been decided as far back as 1967 that the USN and USAF were to team together and invite proposals from engine manufacturers to provide the powerplants for their F-14B (USN) and F-15

F-15B-4-MC 71-0291 seen here wearing FAST packs in the late 1970s. Both the FAST packs and '291 would go on to play crucial parts in the Strike Eagle programme – the former as Conformal Fuel Tanks, the latter as the prototype F-15E. (Boeing via Author)

airframes. The programme went under the name Advanced Turbine Engine Gas Generator (ATEGG). ATEGG drew on experiences learned through the General Electric TF30, the engine which powered the troubled F-111 bomber (and also the F-14A). It included design goals to improve thrust output, reduce weight and achieve a minimum thrust-to-weight ratio of 9:1. General Electric (GE), General Motors and Pratt & Whitney (P&W) were sent RFPs in April 1968. General Motors was deselected from the programme in August the same year, leaving P&W and GE to complete an 18-month contract worth $118 million to decide the winner. On 27 March 1970, a $448 million contract was awarded to P&W to produce 90 F100-PW-100 (USAF designation) and F401-PW-400 (USN designation) engines for test and evaluation. A Joint Engine Project Office (JEPO) had been established to iron out some of the differences that naturally arose as a result of the Navy having slightly different requirements of the engine than the Air Force. (The Navy wanted more thrust than the Air Force, which in turn was happy with less thrust and less frequent overhaul times.)

The flight-rating test was to be completed by February 1972, and the final qualification test in May 1973. The former was necessary to allow the testing programme to start – it ensured that the engine was safe enough for testing to start in earnest. The latter was the real litmus test – it determined the operational suitability of the engine. Both tests were subsequently passed, although the qualification test only came to an end in October 1973 – five months late (as a result of a turbine failure in one of the test engines and problems with the compressor section's efficiency). Simultaneously, the USN threw another problem into the melting pot: it was cutting its proposed order of 179 units to 69. It then further cut this to 58. Project costs escalated as problems continued to frustrate the more complex development cycle for the Navy version of the engine. In June 1971, the Navy cancelled its order for the F401, deciding instead to make more F-14A airframes and to continue using the unreliable and compressor-stall-prone TF30. The cost overruns ballooned as a result. Despite the fact that the Navy was no longer interested in purchasing the engine, each service forfeited $110 million to cover these extra costs.

With the specific requirements of the USN now out of the way, the F100 now employed an advanced aerodynamic compressor (which had been too heavy for the Navy's requirements). The advanced compressor redressed performance problems and deficiencies which had plagued the 'standard' compressor section and had contributed to the delay in completing the qualification test.

Eventually the cost of each engine would fall as units were ordered for the F-16. The USN would have to wait 15 years before replacing the ailing TF30 with the significantly improved F110-GE-400 on some of its fleet of F-14 Tomcats.

Weapons and avionics

It had been decided to internally mount a cannon in the left wing root of McAir model B-199; placing it in the nose could have an adverse effect on the avionics stored in racks behind the radar dome. Philco-Ford had initially provided the GAU-7A for evaluation in December 1971, but technical problems eventually led to the 20-mm GE M61A1 Vulcan cannon being selected in November 1972. Despite the disappointing performance of both the AIM-9 and AIM-7 in Vietnam, the F-15 was to carry four AIM-7 and four AIM-9 missiles as standard; the USAF believed that the problems afflicting these missiles could be remedied to improve their reliability, and also believed that missiles of the future would improve the poor kill ratios seen so far.

Hughes had been awarded the tender to build a radar for the F-X programme in 1968. There

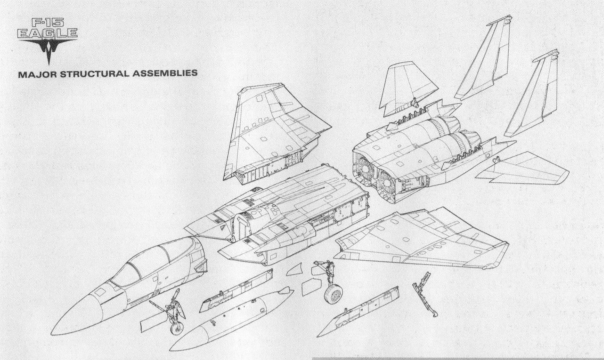

Brochure pictures from McAir showing the composition and material distribution of the F-15A, and that of its major assembly parts. These illustrations aptly demonstrate the manufacturing and technological advances made since the development of the F-4. Despite similar physical dimensions, the F-15 weighed in at a colossal 2722 kg (6,000 lb) lighter than the Phantom. In addition, the F-15 was substantially less time-consuming to assemble. (Boeing via Author)

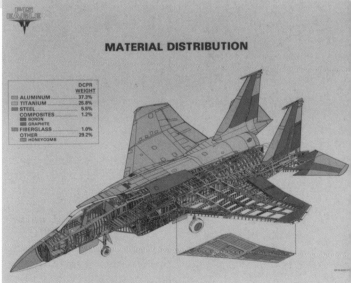

had been several design options, but the one eventually chosen encompassed the following philosophy: to produce an advanced radar with a limited capability against ground threats, an all-weather capability against airborne threats (including AIM-7 guidance provision and 'look-down' capability) and provision for cueing optical tracking systems which may be installed at a later date (as in the F-15E). Chosen by McAir and approved by the USAF, Hughes received an $82 million contract in October 1970 to build what was to become known as the APG-63 radar.

The APG-63 held numerous advantages over the older Westinghouse radar housed in the nose of the F-4. It could track targets in ground clutter using Doppler shift, it could use high and medium pulse repetition frequencies (PRFs) to track targets at different ranges, in formations, and at different closing speeds and locations relative to the itself; and it could interrogate a contact with IFF in order to determine if it was a 'friendly'. In the ground mode it could map the terrain ahead in order to navigate, and update the Inertial Navigation System (INS); it could also provide steering to bomb a ground target designated by the pilot.

The F-15's weapons system was the most sophisticated fielded in any fighter at that time. Garth Granrud recalls that, 'The biggest difference between the F-106 and F-15 was the fire control system, the F-15 had lots of power and sophistication. The weapons system in the F-106 was labour intensive – we had a semblance of HOTAS [Hands on Throttle and Stick] to help out, but it really wasn't as good as the F-15's. We had no AUTO lock modes, everything was done manually and required a lot of "heads down time".'

The first Eagle

F-15A-1-MC, tail number 71-0280, rolled out of McAir's St Louis, Seattle plant on 26 June 1972. Shipped to Edwards AFB in a Lockheed C-5 Galaxy, it made its first flight on 27 July. It flew for 50 minutes with McAir's test pilot Irving L Burrows at the controls. One week later, '280 had already made another four flights, taking it to Mach 1.5 and 13716 m (45,000 ft). Two months later, and with another 40 hours of flying logged, a speed of Mach 2.3 and an altitude of 18288 m (60,000 ft) had been reached.

Testing was broken down into two categories; Category I: Contractor Development Test & Evaluation (CDT&E) which received twelve airframes (71-0280 to 71-0291); and Category II: Air Force Development Test & Evaluation (AFDT&E) with eight airframes (72-0113 to 72-0120) under the F-15 Joint Test Force (JTF).

Despite persistent pressure from Congress and accusations that the F-15 programme was home to a myriad of faults, the testing programmes ran smoothly throughout 1972 and 1973. Modifications to the wing tips were made to alleviate a buffeting problem at high *g*, the speed brake was enlarged to increase its effectiveness at smaller opening angles (in its smaller form it had been required to open almost vertically and this had caused unacceptable buffet), the horizontal stabiliser was modified to eradicate a slight flutter problem, and the landing gear received attention to permit it to handle a 30° crosswind component. In total, these changes numbered just 38, compared to 140 or so made for the F-4.

During the two-year-long testing period, McAir had developed aerodynamically optimised fuel tanks which it called Fuel and Sensor Tactical packs (FAST packs). These packs slotted under the wing and fitted snugly with the fuselage to carry fuel and weapons. The Air Force liked them enough to decree that all F-15s should be produced with the capability of carrying them, and they later formed the basis of the CFT (Conformal Fuel Tanks), which are almost always seen mounted on the F-15E Strike Eagle. As well as carrying fuel, McAir also suggested that they might be used to carry camera and reconnaissance equipment, or even listening and jamming devices to enable the F-15 to act as a 'Wild Weasel' (an aircraft dedicated to attacking and suppressing enemy radar systems). Despite such ingenuity, the Air Force had little time to consider the F-15 in other roles, and these ideas were quietly dropped.

Production innovations

From the outset the F-15 had been designed to be easier to manufacture and maintain. New manufacturing techniques and materials allowed the F-15 to be built in a shorter time period and with less production effort. The F-15's fuselage was simple in construction. It was built from a mere three sections, which assembled to form a whole (which contributed to a 300 per cent longer fatigue life than the F-4). This was a stark contrast to the F-4, where lots of small pieces combined to make a heavy, awkward and labour-intensive fuselage section. By way of illustration, 690,000 production hours had been set aside to build airframes '280 to '285, but McAir managed it in 466,000 hours. Despite being of similar dimensions to the F-4 it was due to replace, simpler manufacturing techniques and lighter materials (such as titanium and composites) made the F-15 considerably lighter.

Opposite: The Israelis debated over the choice between the F-15 and F-16. Eventually they bought both, although the F-16 was purchased in much greater numbers as it was far cheaper. As is evident from this picture and those which follow, the Israelis are especially known for two things: their indigenous modifications to the aircraft they purchase (the F-16 nearest the camera has been converted into a Wild Weasel), and their sense of adventure. (IDF/AF)

2. Operational History

Despite the fact that the F-15 is an extremely versatile platform, the Eagle is not an aircraft that many nations can afford to purchase and maintain. It has been outsold by the F-16 – the quintessentially affordable, multi-role fighter, although Boeing has manufactured 1,365 F-15 airframes for four nations at the time of writing.

Heyl Ha'Avir – IDF/AF

Israel was the first foreign nation to purchase the F-15A. Israel had fought the Six Day War in 1967, the War of Attrition with Syria and Egypt until 1970, and the Yom Kippur War in 1973. In that time it had lost more than 150 aircraft, albeit learning a great deal in the process. A number of choices were on offer when the decision came from Benny Paled, the Israeli Defence Force/Air Force (IDF/AF) Chief of Staff, to replace the attrited airframes of the past six or seven years and to start replacing the F-4 Phantom with a modern, superior airframe. Iran had recently purchased the F-14A Tomcat – the US Navy's equivalent of the F-15. Yet the Tomcat, with its

similar price tag, offered superior long-range interception capabilities and better endurance, on paper at least. In addition to this, the Tomcat's Radar (AWG-9) and weapons (primarily the AIM-54 Phoenix AAM) had been designed to work co-operatively with the Grumman E-2 Hawkeye's AWACS radar and data link system, and the Israelis were going to buy four Hawkeyes. The other alternative was the F-16A, certainly more nimble than the F-15, but less able to loiter due to fuel constraints, and lacking the longer range detection capability of the APG-63. In truth, the IDF/AF wanted to mix and match a combination of airframes; either buy the F-15 or F-14 in limited numbers and then buy the F-16 in greater numbers, thus ensuring that both the 'capability' and 'quantity' check boxes could be ticked. The IDF/AF's priorities were to be able to fight for and gain air superiority, fly deep-interdiction missions and to be able to provide long-range support to troops in contact. The F-15

This two-seat F-15B saddles up to an Israeli C-130 Hercules as part of a photo shoot opportunity. (IDF)

could climb to 9144 m (30,000 ft) and be flying at 0.9 Mach for an intercept in less than 1 minute 30 seconds from take-off, it had excellent low-speed handling characteristics, and its radar, HOTAS and head-up display (HUD) were immediate indicators to the Israelis that in this jet they would hold a significant advantage over their Arab opponents (who were equipped and trained largely by the Soviets).

An order for 25 F-15As was made in 1975, with the first airframes being delivered under the Foreign Military Sales (FMS) programme named *Peace Fox* on 10 December 1976. Although this represented only half of the quantity that the IDF/AF had wanted, it was an expensive purchase; some estimates value the sale at between $24 million and $30 million per aircraft. Interestingly, such was the priority of the IDF/AF order, that four of its airframes came from the Category II Operational Test & Evaluation (OT&E) force. Some 19 brand-new F-15As were delivered to the IDF/AF later on that month as Phase II of *Peace Fox*, and two B-model Eagles arrived in early 1977. The IDF/AF had initially sent six pilots to Edwards AFB in the US to learn to fly and operate the F-15 – this was necessary in view of the lack of adequate training facilities (i.e. a simulator) available in Israel at the time. Upon their return, they embarked on an intensive training programme to bring talented and capable pilots up to speed on the F-15 in as short a time as possible. In all, the F-15 pilots flew training sorties for 18 months before they flew their first combat mission. A few weeks later, the Israelis became the first operator ever to score an air-to-air kill in the F-15. By December 1980, the F-15 had scored 11 Syrian MiG kills in the hands of the IDF/AF. One month later it would score its 12th, and in doing so become the first aircraft ever to shoot down a MiG-25 'Foxbat'. The Heyl Ha'Avir (IDF/AF) modified all of its F-15s to carry the Israeli-built Shafrir IR AAM, as well as Rafael Python 2 and Python 4 advanced IR AAMs. In addition, IAI manufactured CFTs locally. Most of the IDF/AF's F-15 kills have been achieved within visual range (WVR), using IR AAMs.

The IDF/AF gave the F-15A the Hebrew name Baz (falcon); it named its F-16s (which also arrived in 1976) Netz (hawk). The two types worked together in 1981 for Operation *Opera*, an Israeli strike on the nuclear reactor at Tammuz, near Baghdad, Iraq. For years the Israelis had monitored the site and, with a mountain of supporting evidence continuing to build, had concluded that Saddam Hussein, the Iraqi dictator, had been using it to develop nuclear weapons, rather than for its intended purpose. Eight F-16s and eight F-15A escorts ingressed the target on a Sunday afternoon, flying at 61 m (200 ft) over Saudi Arabia from a forward operating base in Israel. The F-16s and F-15s maintained low altitude until reaching their initial point (IP), at which time the F-16s popped up to 1219 m (4,000 ft), rolled inverted, acquired their target visually, placed their continuously-computed impact point (CCIP) pippers over the target and each delivered two (sixteen total) Mk 84 low-drag general purpose (LDGP) bombs. Simultaneously, the escorting F-15s zoom-climbed to 6096 m (20,000 ft) and split into pairs to fly a CAP in order to cover the strikers egress from the target. The strike was successful, although the strike package encountered no opposition – it had caught the Iraqi air defence forces off guard.

It would be remiss not to note that the IDF/AF did receive data link pods and the GBU-15 for its F-15 fleet – these were supplied to provide Israel with a stand-off precision-guided munition (PGM) capability. Although reports would indicate that these weapons have seen little use, it is known that a group of eight F-15Ds struck a PLO barracks in Tunis, flying a 4023-km (2,500-mile) round trip in October 1985.

Peace Fox III took place later in 1981 with the delivery of 18 F-15C Akev (buzzard) aircraft, and eight F-15Ds, to 106 Squadron. One year later the squadron announced that it had attained its initial operating capability (IOC). Israeli versions of the F-15 had always been subject to US export laws, and the F-15C was no different. Some of the Tactical Electronic Warfare System (TEWS) had been deleted by the omission of the ALQ-128 Electronic Warfare Warning System (EWWS) and most likely the ALQ-135 Internal Countermeasures Set (ICS); the nuclear-delivery capability was deleted from the central computer (CC) and bombing computer. The Israeli F-15Cs featured indigenous chaff/flare dispensers and had an IC-7 seat in place of the ACES II. In 1989 *Peace Fox IV* delivered an additional five F-15D two-seaters as attrition replacements.

The last Israeli acquisition of the F-15A came after Operation *Desert Storm*, when the US government offered the IDF/AF 17 ex-Air National Guard (ANG) F-15s at a discounted price. This was by way of thanking Israel for its restraint while on the receiving end of Saddam Hussein's 'Scud' missiles. It is likely that these F-15s were base models and had not received the Multi-Stage Improvement Program II (MSIP II) upgrade; they were 1973/1974 builds.

To date, the IDF/AF has shot down over 56 enemy aircraft (all Syrian) with the F-15, for a loss of not a single machine. Two IDF/AF F-15A/B/C/D squadrons exist: 133rd Squadron flies early-model A and B F-15s, and 106 Squadron, at Tel Nov AB, flies C and D models. The F-15 has a 56.5:0 kill ratio in Israeli service, with several jets scoring multiple kills – F-15C '840 (80-0129) has a total of six Syrian kills to its credit.

The F-15I features a DASH (Display and Sighting Helmet) helmet-mounted display. This system uses electromagnetic fields (generated by a 2000V battery) in the cockpit to determine where the Weapons Systems Operator (WSO) or pilot is looking. Using this system, either crew member can cue sensors (radar, LANTIRN, AAM seekers, etc) onto a target by simply looking at it and pressing a button. The system is said to work equally well against airborne and ground targets. (Steve Davies)

F-15s with the APG-63(V)I radar will often see an F-16 at 64 km (40 miles) or more; the F-16 pilot, on the other hand, may not detect the F-15 until 48 km (30 miles) or so, despite the much larger radar signature of the F-15. Obvious here are the leading edge flaps used by the F-16 to maintain lift at slow speeds, the F-15 is devoid of these leading edge flaps, although it does have single-position, inboard trailing edge flaps. (IDF)

F-15I Ra'am (thunder)

On 27 January 1994, the Israeli government announced that it intended to purchase the F-15I for its long-range, all-weather precision-strike requirement. It had evaluated the F-16, F-15E and F/A-18 for the role, and chose the F-15E (the Eagle variant on which the F-15I is based) despite a failed last-minute attempt by Lockheed's Fort Worth Division (formerly, General Dynamics) to interest it in a new version of the Fighting Falcon – the F-16ES, or Enhanced Strategic. The chosen aircraft was to be tasked with the destruction of 'high quality targets' and was to be able to perform its mission over long ranges and in inclement weather, night or day. With its two-person crew, unsurpassed sensor suite and proven capability, the F-15E was perhaps the ideal choice.

The Israeli order was quickly approved by the US DoD, and a letter of offer and acceptance was signed on 12 May 1994 between the governments of the United States and Israel, authorising McDonnell Douglas to build an initial batch of 21 F-15Is for the IDF/AF (*Peace Fox VI*) plus an option for four more. This option was exercised in November 1995, raising the total to 25. With Boeing taking over McDonnell Douglas in 1997, the first F-15I flight took place at Boeing's

St Louis plant on 12 September 1997, and deliveries began at the rate of one per month in January 1998 to 69 Squadron 'The Hammers', at Hatzerim AB in south west Israel. Details of specific missions flown by the F-15I are scant; however, the Ra'am has seen constant use since reaching IOC in 1999, starting with attacks against terrorist training camps in the Lebanon that same year.

Royal Saudi Air Force

The Royal Saudi Air Force (RSAF) had traditionally relied upon British air defence hardware, but its ageing English Electric Lightning fleet, and the overthrow of the Shah of Iran, had left Saudi Arabia feeling distinctly exposed in the early 1980s. *Peace Sun* was the FMS name given to the sale of the F-15 to Saudi Arabia by the US DoD. The Saudis had initially wanted to purchase the F-14 Tomcat in order to provide both a long-range shield with which to deter the Soviets and also to counter the Iranian Shah's F-14s. Eventually however, the RSAF purchased five E-3A AWACS (delivered in 1982), 46 F-15Cs (minus some TEWS elements and various sensitive radar modes) and sixteen F-15Ds. In order to minimise the tensions that might have resulted between Israel and Saudi Arabia, the US Congress ruled that the supply of CFTs to the RSAF would be limited (to reduce the number of long-range Saudi F-15s), and that no more than 60 F-15s could be operated by the RSAF at any one time; hence two attrition replacements from the order of 62 jets were held in reserve in the US. In 1990, and with some haste, this limit was lifted when Kuwait was invaded by Iraqi forces. An additional 24 aircraft were rushed to the RSAF from front-line United States Air Force in Europe (USAFE) units. It is likely that the Iraqi threat also prompted the US Congress to permit the release of the ALQ-135 ICS, although the ALQ-128 was deleted prior to delivery. Subsequently, the RSAF has had some of its F-15Cs upgraded to MSIP II standard.

The RSAF's Eagles have not seen anywhere near the level of action that their Israeli counterparts have, yet they have been used to full effect when necessary. They are credited with destroying two Iranian F-4Es that penetrated Saudi airspace in June 1984, and with the destruction of two Iraqi Dassault Mirage F1EQs during Operation *Desert Storm*. (Captain Ayehid Salah al-Shamrani of 13 Squadron, RSAF, used two AIM-9Ps to down the Mirages on 19 January 1991.)

F-15S (F-15XP)

The F-15S is the Saudi version of the F-15E. Purchased in May 1993, the deal for 72 of these jets is the largest FMS programme ever, standing at $9 billion. As with the Israeli F-15I deal, LANTIRN (Low-Altitude Targeting by Infra Red at Night) pods were provided, so too were CFTs, spares, training and support. Some reports indicate that the RSAF had dedicated some of its S model airframes to the air-to-air role; the author's interviews with US aircrew who have flown exchange tours with the RSAF suggest that this is not the case.

The following RSAF squadrons operate the F-15C/D: 5 Sqn, King Fahd AFB, Taif; 6 Sqn, King Khaled AFB, Khamis Mushayt; 13 Sqn and 42 Sqn, King Adbdul Aziz AFB, Dharahn and No. 55 Sqn, King Khaled, Khamis Mushayt, flies the F-15S.

Japan Air Self Defence Force

The Japan Air Self Defence Force (JASDF) is the world's largest export customer for the F-15, with a total of 186 F-15J and F-15DJ aircraft, bought under FMS programme *Peace Eagle*. The Japanese first test flew the F-15C and D Eagle in the summer of 1975, as part of an evaluation of thirteen different airframes to fill their Air Superiority fighter requirement. The airframe was to supersede Japan's F-4EJ Phantoms and F-104J Starfighters. The JASDF selected the F-15J and DJ models – almost identical to USAF F-15Cs and Ds respectively, but minus some of the electronic warfare (EW) and nuclear equipment as per the Israeli and Saudi sales. The Japanese government also secured a licence for a conglomerate of Japanese companies to produce the F-15 locally. On 15 July 1980 the first ever F-15J was delivered. Following delivery of the second F-15J a month later, JASDF pilots went on to test the two jets extensively in the US, before ferrying them to Japan for further 'quality assurance' testing.

The JASDF installed its own electronic countermeasures (ECM) systems and a GCI data link system. Some sources suggest that Japan's

52-8847, an F-15J, seen taxiing in the early 1990s. The Japan Air Self Defence Force was meticulous in its evaluation of the F-15. Japanese F-15s were the first in the world to receive a GCI data link. (Masahiro Koizumi via Dennis R. Jenkins)

J/ALQ-8 system is comparable to the AN/ALQ-135 fitted to US F-15s. The F-15J and DJ were originally powered by PW-100 engines; the least-sophisticated and least-powerful of the F100 family of engines. However, 1992 saw the fleet begin a re-engining programme with the F100-PW-220 and, in 1996, to the PW-220E; an improved version of the PW-220.

United States Air Force

The F-15 is most prolific in the service of the United Stated Air Force. Excluding the 20 FSD airframes, the USAF has bought 366 F-15As, 57 F-15Bs, 409 F-15Cs, 61 F-15Ds and 226 F-15Es.

The 1st Fighter Wing (FW), at Langley AFB, Virginia, was the first operational wing to receive the F-15, in January 1976, although the jet had been tested in the hands of the 555th Tactical Fighter Training Squadron (TFTS), of the 58th Tactical Fighter Training Wing (TFTW) at Luke AFB, Arizona since November 1974. Within 12 months, 51 F-15s were flying with the 58th TFTW at Luke AFB, 63 with Langley's 1st Tactical Fighter Wing (TFW), and two with the

This Luke AFB F-15A belongs to the 555th TFTS, better known as the 'Triple Nickel' squadron. The unit fell under the authority of the 58th TFTW. It was commanded by Col Chuck Horner – Horner would later rise to the rank of general, and was the commanding officer in charge of planning and executing the air war during Operation *Desert Storm*. This photo dates to July 1991 and the unit no longer operates the F-15. (Ted Carlson via Steve Davies)

57th Fighter Weapons Wing (FWW) at Nellis AFB, Nevada. These early wings participated in a programme called *Pacer Century* – an accelerated engine reliability and maintainability evaluation designed to quickly wear the engines and to determine a realistic fatigue life for a typical F100. In time, these tests would lead to the increase in F100 fatigue life from 500 to 750 hours.

With an average of nine jets rolling off the St Louis production line each month, 143 aircraft racked up 25,000 flight hours in the first year of service alone. The Eagle was not performing as well as had been anticipated however, and sortie generation rates at Luke AFB had fallen to below half the 1.33 expected per airframe per day. Engine problems were occurring with greater regularity than had originally been foreseen – the engine was proving to be less reliable than had been planned. The mean time between failure (MTBF) rate stood at half of that planned, and the maintenance man hour/flight hour (MMH/FH) of 31 hours was being made up of at least 14 hours of engine trouble shooting. Despite the poor sortie rate of the F-15, the USAF was pleased enough with the F-15 to send it to Europe. In June 1977, 23 Eagles of the 36th TFW flew to Bitburg AB, West Germany. They were to provide air defence to NATO's central front. In preparation, the 1st FW had spent some months running Operation *Ready Eagle*, to provide Bitburg with 88 qualified pilots, 522 maintenance specialists and an additional 1,100 maintenance personnel. In addition to its European presence, the 36th TFW made several overseas deployments in 1978 – the 94th Tactical Fighter Squadron (TFS) deployed eight jets to Kadena, Japan and bases in the Philippines and Korea; the 94th TFS and 71st TFS sent 18 Eagles to the Netherlands. Later, the 53rd FS deployed from Bitburg to Tabuk AB, Saudi Arabia for Operation *Desert Storm*. It is credited with 11 Iraqi aircraft shot down. The 53rd was deactivated in 1994, and its assets and personnel were assigned to the 52nd Wing, Spangdhalem AFB, Germany in 1995 – it was to become the largest fighter wing in the USAFE, employing not only F-15C/D aircraft, but also F-16s and A-10s. The 525th FS was deployed to Incirlik, Turkey, for the Gulf War. It too claimed kills – this time five – it was subsequently deactivated in 1992.

The 57th FWW continued to develop tactics for the F-15, and was provided with an additional twelve airframes in June 1977. It was at this time that the Wing also participated in the Air Intercept Missile Evaluation/Air Combat Evaluation (AIMVAL/ACEVAL) test programme. The programme had been designed to evaluate/prove that BVR fighters carrying medium-range, radar-guided missiles could dominate smaller, WVR type fighters. USAF F-15s and US Navy F-14s flew against small Northrop F-5E Tiger II and T-38 Talon aggressor aircraft flown by hand-picked USAF and Navy fighter pilots. The USAF and USN never released the results of these tests, although it is understood that the F-15 and F-14 won convincingly on nearly every occasion. The 57th FWW went on to become an FW and finally, in 1994, a Wing. It is among the oldest F-15 operators in the USAF. It is currently host to the 422nd Test & Evaluation Squadron, flying F-15Es and F-15Cs at Nellis AFB. The 422nd is responsible for devising and evaluating tactics for the F-15 community, as well as running the F-15E and F-15C Weapons Schools.

F-15 squadrons

The F-15 served extensively in continental Europe, Alaska and Iceland as well as at home in the continental United States (CONUS). Among the least known but highly important squadrons which flew the Eagle were the Fighter Interceptor Squadrons (FISs) – tasked with protecting CONUS from Soviet nuclear bombers. These squadrons had all disbanded by 1991, but were the 48th FIS, Langley AFB (April 1982–September 1991); 318th FIS, McChord AFB (1983); 186th FIS, Montana ANG (February 1988–December 1999); and the 123rd FIS at Portland, Oregon.

Garth Granrud was the Operations Director at Langley's 48th FIS in the late 1970s, and flew many Tupolev Tu-95 'Bear' intercepts in that capacity. He recounts the 'Zulu alert' mission the Squadron was required to fulfil: 'Hours and hours of boredom! We would usually have two aircraft sitting in the alert barn at the end of the runway. We'd cock the jets [set the switches ready for a quick start] and waited for the signal to go. The limiting factor in the speed at which we could go was the early mechanical INS [the F-15

'WA' tail-coded F-15D with gear extended prior to final approach to its home airfield, Nellis AFB, in January 1992. The 57th developed tactics for the F-15 community over a number of years and it holds the distinction of being the Wing chosen to run the AIMVAL/ACEVAL exercises. (Ted Carlson via Steve Davies)

would later receive Ring Laser Gyros]. When the call came, we would start the jet, align the INS, taxi and make a priority rolling take-off in as short a time as possible. We'd carry four AIM-9s and four AIM-7s, and once airborne, usually flying in pre-arranged corridors where we'd be cleared and unrestricted [to fly fast without fear of mid-air collision with other aviation traffic], we'd be passed from Departure [air traffic control at the base] to the Air Defense Unit [ADU]. They'd give us our target or intercept co-ordinates. For practice, which usually happened about twice a week, they'd give us CAP stations and then vectored targets in towards us. When a real alert came, as it often did when the Soviets flew large-scale exercises, we'd be required to make sure they did not penetrate the ADIZ [Air Defence Identification Zone]. During the day time the intercepts were quite routine, we'd fly up to them and keep them away from the ADIZ. Sometimes they would wave and we would wave back. At night, in winter, it was a different story! I certainly heard stories of them being aggressive towards some of the F-15s in Iceland [Keflavik]. It was said that they flew low and tried to rake our guys into the water, or that they'd turn hard into them, but I never saw it myself. More often than not we'd fly most of our intercepts in October – the Soviets would fly down to Cuba for the winter! On the way there they would fly straight in as they were low on fuel, but once there, they would test our defences and reaction times. We knew from their flight

profile where they were going to go; sometimes low and up the east coast, sometimes higher and along to the west. We'd shadow them all the way – one ADU would hand them off to another. There was only one time that I can remember where they got by unnoticed.'

Alaska's Elmendorf AFB, has been home to the 3rd Wing's F-15A/B/C/Ds since 1988, with the 19th FS and 54th FS operating in the harsh winter climes. CFTs are often installed on 'AK' (Elmendorf tail code) F-15C/Ds, as they provide additional fuel reserves in the event that weather forces a diversion. The 'AK' Eagles are tasked with the protection of Alaska and some local parts of Canada – like the 'IS' (Keflavik AB) F-15s, the 19th FS and 54th FS are responsible for intercepting unknown and hostile aircraft. Alaska is also home to twenty or so F-15Es of the 90th FS. First arriving in 1990, the Strike Eagles at Elmendorf today are among the older jets in the F-15E inventory.

F-15s from the 57th FS, Keflavik Naval Station (NS), Iceland, which also regularly carry CFTs, arrived in July 1985. Originally assigned to intercept and escort stray Soviet aircraft, F-15Cs were still intercepting reconnaissance and bomber aircraft from Keflavik as recently as 1999. Amid tensions between the CIS and NATO following NATO's actions in the Balkans region, two Tu-95MS 'Bear-H' nuclear bomber aircraft flew within striking distance of the United States before being turned back by 159th TFW, Louisiana ANG F-15s on deployment.

Norwegian air force F-16s then intercepted the 'Bears' as they approached Europe on their return home. One of the 57th's busiest years was 1985, when it intercepted over 170 'transients'.

Kadena AFB, Japan, has been home to the F-15C/D since 1979. Eagles are operated by the 18th Fighter Wing's 12th FS, 67th FS and 44th FS. Kadena Eagles wear the 'ZZ' tail code, and regularly 'mix it up' with Japanese F-15 aggressor squadrons. On a more serious note, the 18th FW is responsible for providing 'Alert' Eagles to cover the Korean peninsula.

The F-15E first entered operational service with the 4th FW at Seymour Johnson AFB in 1989. Leaving its F-4Es behind, the Wing had completed its transition to the F-15E by July 1991. The Wing would eventually consist of the 333rd FS, 334th FS, 335th FS and 336th FS. The 336th FS was the first to reach IOC in October 1989, a year later to the day, the 335th FS gained its IOC rating, followed by the 334th in July 1991. The 333rd FS was only activated in 1994, and alongside the

57th FS F-15s were based at Iceland's Keflavik Air Base. As demonstrated in this 1992 photograph of F-15C 80-0048, they ordinarily operated with CFTs installed as a precaution in case of the need to divert – if Keflavik's runway was closed they would have to fly 700 nm (1297 km; 806 miles) to Scotland! The 'IS' tail code is often associated with 'Bear' intercepts; reports suggest that some of these intercepts were greeted with aggressive behaviour from the Soviets. (Ted Carlson)

Two 114th FS, 173rd FW F-15 Eagles from Kingsley Field ANGB, Oregon, fly a training mission over northern California's Mount Shasta. Furthest from the camera is a B-model Eagle. (USAF)

334th is a training squadron. It was the 336th FS which provided the bulk of the crews and airframes for Operation *Desert Storm*, although they were reinforced later on in the conflict by the 335th FS. 'SJ' crews from both operational squadrons have served deployments to the Persian Gulf region as part of Operations *Northern Watch* and *Southern Watch*. In fact, all four operational F-15E squadrons rotate in and out of these operations on a three-monthly, pre-planned basis, as Air Expeditionary Forces (AEFs). The 4th TFW(P) was a provisional wing formed for Operation *Desert Storm*; it was the operating wing for the Saudi Arabia-based Strike Eagles.

RAF Lakenheath, England, plays host to the 48th FW. The 'Statue of Liberty Wing' is among the most important wings in the USAF. It comprises F-15Cs of the 493rd FS, and F-15Es of the 492nd FS and 494th FS. The Strike Eagles came to the 48th FW in 1992, replacing the much loved F-111F. Lakenheath's F-15Es tend to be the most modern, and, unlike those at Seymour Johnson AFB, are powered exclusively by the higher-thrust PW-229 motor. Like other F-15 Wings, all three 'LN' squadrons play their part not only in AEF deployments, but also in impromptu operations such as *Deliberate Force*, when in 1995 F-15Es flew attack sorties against elements of the Bosnian-Serb ground forces. 'LN' F-15Es used the GBU-15 glide bombs for the first time ever with great success during this time. More recently, the 48th FW has sent aircraft to Incirlik, Turkey as part of Operation *Provide Comfort*, and has supported *Enduring Freedom*; F-15Es flew escort for Boeing C-17 Globemaster

Left: Seymour Johnson AFB, North Carolina, is home to the 4th FW. Four squadrons of F-15E Strike Eagles fall under the 4th FW's command; one of these (333rd FS) is the Fighter Training Unit, which is responsible for teaching every USAF F-15E WSO and pilot. The 4th FW (P) was the first offensive strike contingent to deploy to the Gulf region during Operation *Desert Shield*. (Ted Carlson)

Above and above right: The 48th FW has been resident at RAF Lakenheath, England, since its first F-100D touched down on RAF Lakenheath's runway on 15 January 1960. In the time that has elapsed since, the Wing has participated in numerous combat operations, including Operation *El Dorado Canyon* (the 1986 strike against Libya), Operation *Desert Storm*, Operations *Deny Flight* and *Allied Force*, Operations *Northern* and *Southern Watch*, and Operation *Enduring Freedom*. These photographs show the Wing Commander's F-15E and an F-15D of the 493rd FS – the Wing's 'light gray' Eagle operator. (Steve Davies)

Perhaps the most famous Eagles in the world are those which carry the 'EG' tail code. This example, F-15C 85-0122 was flown by Capt. Craig Underhill when it engaged and dispatched an Iraqi MiG-29 on the third day of Operation *Desert Storm*. Subsequently repainted in the darker 'Mod Eagle' paint scheme, it carries a green star 'kill' marking on the left forward fuselage. (David F. Brown via the Mick Roth Collection)

IIIs dropping humanitarian aid, and also flew attack sorties using PGMs. The 493rd FS is credited with four MiG-29 kills during 1999's Operation *Allied Force*.

Also based in Europe was the 32nd FS, Camp New Amsterdam, Soesterberg, Netherlands. Although disbanded in 1994, this squadron achieved a single kill during *Desert Storm*, and was under the direct control of NATO while not deployed to Incirlik AB, Turkey.

Although now the USAF's only Lockheed F-117 Nighthawk wing, the 49th FW was an operator of the F-15 from 1977 to 1992. It relieved elements of the 33rd FW post Operation *Desert Storm*, and was based at Holloman AFB, New Mexico ('HO' tail codes).

'EG' tail codes are instantly synonymous with the F-15 for many aviation enthusiasts. Adorning the 'light gray' Eagles of the 33rd FW, the 'EG' Eagles are based in Florida at Eglin AFB. The 33rd FW has been operating the F-15C/D since February 1983, and is the only wing in the USAF to have been the victor at the William Tell Weapons Meet on two consecutive occasions. More interestingly, however, 'EG' Eagles of the 58th FS achieved 13 air-to-air kills during the Gulf War – the highest of any individual participating squadron. The 60th FS recorded a single kill.

The 56th FW is part of Air Education & Training Command, 19th Air Force. It combined the 405th Tactical Training Wing (TTW) (F-15E) with the 58th FW (F-15 training wing) in 1991. Based at Luke AFB, Arizona, the Wing was eventually disbanded in 1995. It was decided to integrate F-15E Replacement Training Unit (RTU) with the 4th Wing at Seymour Johnson. The 461st TFTS was disbanded a year prior to this, in 1994. Previously, the 58th FW (or, 58th TTW as it was known then) had been the principal RTU for the F-15 during the very earliest days of its service. The 405th TTW was initially the F-15E RTU (the 461st TFTS received its first 'Mud Hen' (F-15E) on 1 August 1987, but deactivated in 1992; the 550th TFTS received its first F-15E on 12 May 1989, and the 555th TFTS its first machine in late 1992).

The 366th Wing is an 'air intervention' composite wing formed in 1991. The word 'composite' refers to the fact that the 366th operates several different airframe types, destined to deploy together in the event of conflict, to provide a self-sufficient, flexible, effective fighting force. Thus, the Wing consists of the 391st FS flying the F-15E, the 389th FS with the F-16C, the 34th Bomb Squadron operating B-1Bs, the 390th FS with F-15Cs, and the 22nd ARS (Air Refuelling Squadron) with KC-135R Stratotankers. Demonstrating the concept to maximum effect, the Wing soon made two *Bright*

27

Star deployments to Egypt. Thereafter, it endured the largest operational readiness inspection (ORI) in USAF history when it deployed to Canada. The Wing demonstrated its prowess for real in 1996, when it forward deployed to Turkey in support of *Provide Comfort*. A year later it was playing its part in Operation *Southern Watch*.

The following units have operated the F-15:

1st FW, Langley AFB, Virginia
27th, 71st, 94th FS
Converted to F-15A/B in 1975 and to F-15C/D in early 1980s

3rd Wing, Elmendorf AFB, Alaska
43rd (F-15A and C), 54th (F-15C), 90th (F-15E) FS
Originally designated 21st Composite Wing
Converted to F-15A/B in 1982

4th Wing, Seymour Johnson AFB, North Carolina
334th, 335th, 336th FS
Converted from F-4E to F-15E in 1989–91
Participated in *Desert Storm*

18th FW, Kadena AB, Okinawa, Japan
12th, 44th, 67th FS
Converted to F-15C/D from F-4D in 1979

32nd FS, Soesterberg, Netherlands
Directly under NATO control.

Received first F-15A/Bs in 1978, later re-equipped with F-15C/D.
Participated in *Desert Storm*

33rd FW, Eglin AFB, Florida
58th, 59th, 60th FS
Converted to F-15A/B in 1978, to F-15C/D in 1979–80, then back to F-15A/B in 1980. It reconverted to F-15C/D in 1983
Participated in *Desert Storm*

36th FW, Bitburg AB, West Germany
22nd and 65th FS, 525th TFS
Received F-15A/B in 1977, later re-equipped with F-15C/D
Participated in *Desert Storm*
525th TFS was deactivated in 1992

48th FW, RAF Lakenheath, UK
492nd, 493rd, 494th FS
492nd and 493rd converted from F-111F to F-15E in 1992, 493rd FS converted from F-111F to F-15C in 1992

49th FW, Holloman AFB, New Mexico
7th, 8th, 9th FS
Converted to F-15A/B in 1977
Last USAF unit to operate the F-15A/B
9th FS deployed to Saudi Arabia for *Desert Storm*
Deactivated 1991–92

As a composite wing, the 366th Wing consists of several squadrons operating a range of aircraft. As part of this smorgasbord of aircraft types, the 391st FS operates the F-15E and the 390th FS operates the F-15C. The photograph above shows two 'Bold Tigers' F-15Es flying as part of exercise *Bright Star*. This was used to test the Wing's ability to forward deploy as a single fighting force. Its KC-135, B-1B, F-16 and F-15 aircraft deployed to Egypt, whereupon they conducted joint training operations with the Egyptian air force in 1993 and 1995.

Braving the winter climes, an F-15D of the 3rd Wing awaits ground crew inspection prior to take-off. The 3rd Wing operates two F-15C/D squadrons and one of F-15Es. The F-15Es were heavily involved in Operation *Provide Comfort* in 1995, when it flew escort missions for US and British Lockheed C-130 Hercules dropping aid to Kurdish refugees in Iraq. (Paul F. Crickmore via Steve Davies)

57th FWW, Nellis AFB, Nevada
422nd Test Evaluation Squadron (TES), 433rd FWS
Test and evaluation unit for fighter weapons and tactics
Received F-15A/B in 1977, and F-15C/D in early 1980s

58th Tactical Training Wing (Tactical Fighter Training Wing before 1 April 1977), Luke AFB, Arizona
461st, 550th, 555th TFTS
First unit to receive F-15A/B (1974)
Terminated training in 1979 and transferred its mission to 405th TTW

325th FW, Tyndall AFB, Florida
1st, 2nd, 95th FS
Activated in 1981 as RTU for Tactical Air Command (TAC) and Air National Guard (ANG) F-15s
First F-15A/Bs received in 1983

405th TTW, Luke AFB, Arizona
461st, 550th, 555th TFTS
Activated in 1979 as TAC's RTU for F-15A/B

Converted to F-15E in 1987

1st Air Force (AF), Langley AFB, Virginia
Acquired F-15A/B in early 1980s for air defense role
5th, 48th, 57th, 318th FIS
5th at Minot AFB, North Dakota
Received first F-15A/B in 1985, replacing the F-106A
Deactivated 1985, aircraft sent to Massachusetts ANG.
48th at Langley AFB, Virginia
Received first F-15A/B in 1981/82, replacing the F-106A
Deactivated 1991, aircraft sent to Missouri ANG
57th at Keflavik, Iceland
Converted to F-15C/D from F-4E in 1985
318th at McChord AFB, Washington
Converted to F-15A/B from F-106A in 1983
Deactivated 1989, aircraft sent to Oregon ANG

3246th Test Wing (TW), Eglin AFB, Florida
2347th Test Squadron (TS)

6510th TW, Edwards AFB, California
6512th TS

Two F-15Cs of the 67th FS, 18th FW, Kadena AB, near the coast of Naha, Okinawa, Japan. (USAF)

Tactical Air Warfare Center, Eglin AFB, Florida
4485th TS
F-15A/Bs later replaced by F-15C/D

3246th TW, Air Force Matériel Command, Eglin AFB, Florida
2347th TS
Operates F-15C/D and F-15Es

6510th TW, Edwards AFB, California
6512th TS
Operates F-15C/D and F-15Es

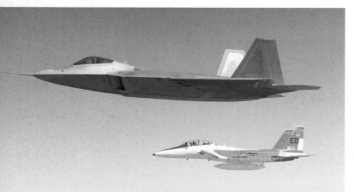

An F-15B of the 415th FLTS at Edwards AFB in 1999. Edwards F-15s are used for a variety of purposes, including chase-ship duties during testing of new airframes, such as here with the F-22. (USAF)

The following ANG organisations used the McDonnell Douglas F-15 Eagle:

102nd Fighter Interceptor Group (FIG)
101st FIS, Massachusetts ANG
First F-15A/Bs received in 1987, replacing F-106A
116th TFW
128th TFS, Georgia ANG
First F-15A/Bs received in 1986, Wing converted from F-4D

150th Tactical Fighter Group (TFG)
188th TFS, New Mexico ANG
Converted to F-15A/B in 1991

159th TFG
122nd TFS, Louisiana ANG

131st TFW
110th TFS, Missouri ANG
Converted to F-15A/B from F-4E in 1991

142nd FIG
123rd FIS, Oregon ANG
Converted to F-15A/B in 1989/90
Aircraft sourced from the disbanded 318th FIS, McChord AFB

154th Composite Group (CG)
199th FIS, Hawaii ANG
F-15A/Bs from 21st TFW replaced F-4C Phantoms in 1987
In mid-1991, F-15Cs were received

3. US Combat Operations

While the Israelis honed their skills and scored MiG kills on a regular basis, US-based Eagle pilots maintained their skills through regular exercises, deployments and inspections for the first 15 years of the type's service. But for one man – Saddam Hussein – things would have stayed the same for several more years to come. On 1 August 1990, Hussein's troops marched into Kuwait; encountering little resistance as they went, they pillaged and looted the city while simultaneously laying claim to it on historical grounds. The response form the United States and its allies was to create and execute Operation *Desert Shield* – the precursor to Operation *Desert Storm*. *Desert Shield*'s first directive was the deployment of 120 USAF and USAFE (USAF Europe) F-15s to Saudi Arabia.

The 1st FW at Langley AFB sent twenty-four F-15C and 3 F-15D aircraft to Dhahran AB, Saudi Arabia, on 7 August 1990. These aircraft, from the 71st TFS, proceeded to operate under the

The oldest fighter wing in the USAF was chosen to lead America's deployment to the Persian Gulf. The 1st FW, from Langley AFB was the first unit to arrive in Saudi Arabia in August 1990. It claimed a single MiG kill during the war. The F-15C illustrated (83-0017, flown by Capt. Steve Tate, downed a Mirage F1EQ on the opening night. (Pat Martin via the Mick Roth Collection)

Air-to-air refuelling was the key to ensuring that the F-15Cs could sweep the area ahead of the strike packages. The F-15 has a modest range on internal and external fuel, but the sorties flown on the first night called for a transit of up to three hours before reaching the assigned CAP points. (Paul F. Crickmore via Steve Davies)

The planners in the Tactical Air Control Center (TACC) in Riyadh, feared that the Iraqi ground forces might try to bulldozer through the northern Saudi oil fields. In anticipation of this, they assigned the 4th TFW's newly acquired F-15E Eagles to fly to Oman, from where they might be able to fly sorties to hinder the advance of any Iraqi armour. The 336th TFS 'The Rocketeers', and some crews from the 335th TFS left Seymour Johnson AFB in the afternoon of 8 August. Amid heavy rain and scenes of farewell from loved ones, they left the runway with travel pods, AIM-9Ls and AIM-7s for the 15-hour non-stop journey to Thumrait, Oman. The 335th TFS would later join the war effort, flying from Al Kharj, Saudi Arabia having worked hard to achieve its own IOC. Eventually, when the immediate threat of an Iraqi armoured advance into Saudi Arabia had subsided, the 336th TFS relocated to Al Kharj.

The TACC had put together a 600-page document called the Air Tasking Order. This ATO was the route map for the air campaign against Iraq. It detailed every sortie, each tanker that was to support it, target arrival times, which targets were to be hit, which munitions to use, what call signs to use and literally hundreds of other vital pieces of information that each strike package would have to know by heart. The F-15Cs were to fly CAP sorties for the 'strikers' as they ingressed their targets, the F-15Es were to fly sorties in unison with F-4G Wild Weasels and EF-111A jammers against SAM sites and key airfield complexes. Despite aggressive training by all 150 or so Eagles, only a single jet was lost: F-15E 87-0203. This aircraft had been flying intercepts against an RAF Jaguar when it ploughed into the desert on 30 September with the loss of its pilot, Maj. Pete Hook and its WSO, Capt. Jim Poulet. It is likely that inexperience at handling the F-15E with three fuel tanks caused the fatal mishap; the pilot misjudged the altitude required to make a stern conversion on the 'Jag' by means of rolling inverted and pulling through 180°.

revised title of 1st TFW (P), 14th Air Division (P). The next day, 25 F-15C/Ds arrived from the 27th TFS to reinforce the assets already on hand. Later, the 58th TFS, 38th TFW, from Eglin AFB, Florida, deployed to King Faisal AB, Saudi Arabia. So too did the 60th TFS – the 'Fighting Crows'. Bitburg AB contributed 24 F-15Cs from the 53rd TFS, while the 525th TFS (Bitburg's other Eagle unit) flew from Incirlik AB in Turkey for the operation. The 32nd TFS, Soesterberg AB, in the Netherlands later joined it, arriving on the first day of the war – 17 January 1991. With these squadrons in place, the USAF believed itself to be acceptably equipped to deal with the anticipated Iraqi air force (IAF) threat. This consisted of the latest MiG-29 fighters, as well as older, but equally worrying, MiG-25, MiG-23 and Mirage F1EQ fighters.

On 17 January, 1991, the order for the first strikes was given by President Bush – Operation *Desert Storm* had begun. With great media attention focused on Baghdad, waves of Grumman A-6 Intruders, Vought A-7 Corsair IIs, Boeing B-52 Stratofortresses, EF-111s, F-14s, F-15Cs, F-15Es, F-16s, F-111Fs, McDonnell Douglas F/A-18 Hornets and Panavia Tornado GR.Mk 1s attacked the 'eyes' and 'ears' of the Iraqi military machine. General Horner, who had taken the 'Checkmate' plans drawn up by a Pentagon think tank and applied them to this conflict, reasoned that by killing the Iraqi air defence system (IADS) and taking out airfields, hardened aircraft shelters (HASs) and aircraft, he could swiftly clinch air superiority. With this in hand, he could then send strike aircraft to decimate Iraqi armour, C^3 (Command, Control & Communications) and logistics supplies, thus paving the way for a less-protracted (and, hopefully, less-bloody) ground war to rid Kuwait of its uninvited guests.

In the events which unfolded that first night, the USAF scored six kills against the Iraqi air force (and another two were scored by USN F/A-18 Hornets), all of them at the hands of the F-15C. Horner's plan had prescribed that a 'wall' of 20 F-15Cs would sanitise the airspace ahead of the strike elements (clear it of Iraqi fighters). It had been anticipated that despite poor training and a dislike for night flying, the Iraqis would hold the MiG-29s for defence of Baghdad and pour hordes of Mirage F1EQs and MiG-23s into the air to repel the 30+ coalition strike packages on their way north that first night. In addition, there was real concern that MiG-25s would be used to make high altitude, high-speed attacks on tankers and AWACS aircraft. The F-15s were to be inserted between Iraqi airspace and coalition forces, and were therefore to be extremely busy. Two flights of four F-15Cs each from the 58th TFS (call signs CITGO and PENNZOIL) were the first to launch. They reached the Iraqi border at 0300Z following some nearly catastrophic refuelling. Horrendous thunder and storm clouds had towered up to 9144 m (30,000 ft) on that pitch black night, putting them and the tankers in turbulent and unpredictable air.

As CITGO flight fanned out and headed north, Eagles from the 36th TFW and 1st TFW followed

shortly after. PENNZOIL soon received a frantic call from AWACS – a strike group of F-15Es was being targeted by MiG-29s. With a mass of friendly contacts filling his radar screens, Capt. Rick 'Kluso' Tollini picked up the bandits at 25 nm (46 km; 28 miles). Almost at the same instant, Capt. John 'JB' Kelk (flying as the element lead) was locked up by an enemy air intercept (AI) system. In the ensuing engagement, Kelk loosed an AIM-7 and downed a MiG-29 just as he closed to within 10 nm (18.5 km; 11 miles) of the contact – the American Eagle had finally bloodied its talons. Meanwhile, CITGO flight was ingressing towards Mudaysis, a small air base with an 'alert' component of three Mirage F1EQs. As the Mirages scrambled to intercept the oncoming rush of Coalition jets, Capt. Rory Graeter engaged two of them. He fired a single AIM-7 Sparrow inside of 10 nm, the lead Mirage exploding soon after, as the missile found its target. In a desperate attempt to avoid the same fate as his leader, the Iraqi wingman began evasive manoeuvring. He flew into the ground while in the process, and so Graeter had scored his second kill. The third Mirage went supersonic and managed to escape Lt Scott Maw. Maw had targeted 'the trailer' while his Flight

John Kelk scored the first kill in a US F-15 when he downed a MiG-29 with an AIM-7 in F-15C 85-0125. Now part of the 3rd Wing, Elmendorf AFB, Alaska, '0125 was owned at the time by the 58th TFS. Today it carries a green MiG-29 kill marking to remind those who fly it that it is no 'ordinary' Eagle! (Jason Passmore via Steve Davies)

Lead had dispatched the two other Mirages, but was unable to close for an AIM-7 missile shot.

As CITGO and PENNZOIL flights checked in and returned to their CAP stations, Capt. Steve Tate of the 71st TFS led his own four-ship package, QUAKER 1, as the eastern element of the wall. The four jets separated into pairs – one flew a high CAP over Al Jawah AB and the other a low CAP to engage any scrambled bogies. Despite an erroneous vector from an AWACS to a bogey that turned out to be an F-111, Tate soon locked up a Mirage F1EQ. With the identification friend or foe (IFF) system and the Enhanced Identification System (EID) confirming that the bogey was in fact a bandit, he swiftly pickled off an AIM-7M while still 12 nm (22 km; 14 miles) distant. The F1 exploded in a ball of flame that stretched across the sky for 400 m (440 yards). Tate regrouped and returned to the tanker.

Throughout the Gulf War, the F-15C found itself in similar situations to that described above, although the IAF soon stopped offering any resistance at all, and eventually focused on survival – many of the remaining combat jets fled to the relative safety of Iran (which, once the war had ended, refused to return them). Indeed, the TACC made the decision later in the war to allocate fighters to fly three separate CAP stations on the Iran/Iraq border. Some Iraqi fighters did manage to make it through however; they waited until there was a break in the coverage (fighter assets were not always at their stations on time) before setting off for the short, adrenaline-pumping, sprint to Iran. AWACS traces of the escaping IAF aircraft, often led to the conclusion that many of those which made it past the CAP stations crashed shortly after making it into Iran. It is likely that fuel starvation was the cause of this.

On 17 January, Capt. Chuck 'Sly' Magill led UNION flight, a group of 16 Eagles attached to a strike force of almost 50 other coalition aircraft tasked to hit two Iraqi air bases (Al Taqaddum and Al Assad). It was the first daylight sortie of the war for the F-15C. Crossing the border at 9144 m (30,000 ft), eight F-15s vectored in on two MiG-29s, flying a slow and repetitive CAP track just south of the airfields. Satisfied that there were only two MiGs, Magill released his second fourship flight to head north west and monitor the airspace above Al Assad. He then closed in on the MiGs, which had begun to accelerate in order to intercept a distant gaggle of USN F-14As. At 20 nm (37 km; 23 miles) the 'Fulcrums' turned their noses towards the four Eagles, and were, in turn, locked up by Magill

Lt Robert Hehemann claimed two Su-25 attack aircraft while flying F-15C 84-0019. Robert Hehemann went on to claim a third kill while flying wing for Capt. Thomas Dietz. Dietz downed a Sukhoi Su-22 'Fitter' while Hehemann manoeuvred in to engage a Pilatus PC-9 turboprop trainer. The PC-9 pilot ejected without a shot being fired. Simultaneously, Dietz and Hehemann became the *Desert Storm's* joint equal highest scoring pilots. (Terry Panopalis Collection via Dennis R. Jenkins)

F-15C 85-0102 was the platform used by both Capt. David Rose and Capt. Anthony Murphy to make their kills. Rose destroyed a MiG-23 on 29 January 1991. Murphy scored a double kill when he engaged Su-22s with AIM-7 Sparrows, some nine days later. Called *Gulf Sprit*, 85-0102 is shown here with three of its own kill markings below a separate kill marking for Col Rick Parsons – Parsons claimed his own Su-22 while flying lead for Murphy in F-15C 85-0124. (Kenneth Kula via the Mick Roth Collection)

and his wingman, Capt. Rhory 'Hoser' Draeger. Magill launched two AIM-7M Sparrows at the lead MiG; Draeger launched a single AIM-7M at the second MiG. With the merge fast approaching, both 'Fulcrums' disintegrated as the three SARH missiles scored direct hits; the F-15s were 2 nm (3.7 km; 2.3 miles) away, close enough for their pilots to visually identify (VID) the MiGs as 'Fulcrums' and to visually authenticate the kills.

On 19 January two more MiG-29s were added to the list when Capt. Craig 'Mole' Underhill and Capt. Caesar 'Rico' Rodriguez fired AIM-7s while flying a high value asset CAP (HVACAP) for KC-10s and an E-3C AWACS. The HVAs were themselves not in jeopardy, but AWACS had called the 'Fulcrums' out as being a threat to a strike package. One MiG-29 was destroyed by a direct AIM-7 Sparrow hit. The other, in an almost carbon copy of events two days before, flew into the ground while evasively manoeuvring. Tollini was once again in the mix of things when he led another CITGO flight of F-15Cs to protect F-15Es, which were searching for the illusive mobile 'Scud' launchers. Within a short while, Tollini and his wingman, Capt. Larry 'Cherry'

Pitts, were being advised of a low flying group of bogies headed straight for them. The bogies turned out to be bandits – MiG-25 'Foxbats'. Flying at supersonic speed a mere 152 m (500 ft) above the sand, the lead 'Foxbat' was attempting to fly behind Tollini's three-nine line (an imaginary line to either side of the aircraft at its '3 o'clock' and '9 o'clock' positions, marking the trailing edge of the pilot's 180° field of view when facing forwards). In doing this, he was trying to take advantage of the APG-63's reliance on doppler shift for target detection and of the limited azimuth in which the radar can scan. But the plan had failed; CITGO flight had manoeuvred so that it maintained the MiGs just at the edge of their radars' horizontal coverage. Turning into the 'Foxbat', Tollini unleashed two AIM-7s and two AIM-9s before the MiG pilot ejected. That same day, two F-15Cs from the 525th TFS bagged two Mirage F1EQ's (the F-15s were crewed by Capt. David S. Prather and Lt David G. Sveden). On 27 January, the RSAF claimed its first (and only) kills of the conflict when a single F-15C intercepted and dispatched another two Mirages .

On 26 January Capt. Rhory 'Hoser' Draeger, and his wingman, Capt. Tony 'Kimo' Schiavi, each downed a MiG-23 'Flogger' with AIM-7 Sparrows. Four 'Floggers' were attempting to escape to a base further north (which was protected by the reach of the SAM ring around Baghdad). One MiG-23 returned to base with a technical problem, but the others were eventually picked up by AWACS and the F-15s. Draeger closed the gap from 100 nm (185 km; 115 miles) to 20 nm (37 km; 23 miles) in a dramatic supersonic chase. Also part of this sortie was Rodriguez, already with two kills to his credit, 'Rico's' AIM-7 had caught the third escaping 'Flogger' moments after the two lead MiG-23s ploughed into the desert with no sign of ejection after being hit by Draeger's missiles.

In the coming weeks, Capt. Jay 'Op' Denney and Capt. Ben 'Coma' Powell destroyed two Iraqi fighters each (three MiG-23s and a Mirage F1EQ); Capt. Don 'Muddy' Watrous downed a MiG-23; Capt. Greg Masters dispatched an Ilyushin Il-76 'Candid' transport; Capt. David Rose destroyed a MiG-23; Capt. Thomas N. Dietz killed two MiG-21s; Lt Robert Hehemann shot down two Su-25 'Frogfoot' attack aircraft; and

three Su-22 attack jets were shot down by Capt. Tony Murphy and Col Rick Parsons (two and one kills respectively). Two helicopter kills came from Capt. Mark McKenzie and Capt. Steve Dingy (who shared an unidentified helo kill) and from Maj. Randy W May, who killed a Mil Mi-24 'Hind' gunship with two AIM-7 Sparrows.

Desert Storm was the real proving ground for the F-15 as far as the USAF was concerned. The conflict demonstrated, conclusively, that the Eagle was a weapons platform of superior capability. It is no secret that the IAF was simply no match for the Coalition – it lacked the inclination and guidance to fight, and when it did make a stand, it demonstrated lack of training and competency in almost every area. It proved, beyond the hypothetical (albeit, accurate) results of *Red Flag* exercises and years of training, that the F-15 could do what it had been designed to do. Electronic wizardry and superior planning had permitted the classification and identification of radar contacts at the very early stages of an engagement; good radar, good missiles and TEWS had allowed the F-15 to fight the battle on its own terms – in some cases to even play with its prey until it was ready to kill. The USAF was very concerned about the MiG-29 – it was certainly a worthy opponent in the WVR arena, and its passive infra red search and track (IRST) system was a technology to which many an F-15 driver gave due consideration. Yet, even though the Iraqi pilots lacked the training and tactical savvy to fully exploit the 'Fulcrum's' capabilities, the F-15 community could take heart from the knowledge that, provided that in future conflicts it could stay out of the MiG's short-range IR missile envelope, the Eagle would hold the upper hand.

Moving mud

While the 'light gray' F-15Cs dealt with the Iraqi air threat, their siblings at Al Kharj were dealing with an entirely different tactical problem altogether. The first nights of the war had seen the ATO task F-15Es with the destruction of key Iraqi airfields and with fixed 'Scud' sites. Iraq achieved very little of military importance during the Gulf War, and launching 'Scuds' was not among those things worth mentioning. Yet the persistent launch of 'Scuds' into Israel was of significant political value – drawing Israel into

The F-15E was a brand-new aircraft at the time of Operations *Desert Shield* and *Desert Storm*. Some crews had only recently transitioned to it from the F-4E or RF-4C Phantom. LANTIRN was new too, and limited numbers of pods were available. What the Strike Eagle crews lacked in experience and equipment, they made up for in enthusiasm and ingenuity. (Ted Carlson via Steve Davies)

the war might have had unimaginable consequences for all concerned.

The fixed 'Scud' sites had been easy enough to strike. F-15Es would ingress the target area at low level at night (medium-altitude deliveries were flown in daylight hours) and at 540 kt (1000 km/h; 620 mph) airspeed. Nearing the target, they would 'pop up', and, using the APG-70's synthetic aperture radar (SAR) mode, would take patch maps of the target. The square, fenced off 'Scud' sites appeared clearly on one of the four screens in the WSO's cockpit. The WSO now had to identify the correct target and designate it with the radar cross-hairs – the computer would then calculate weapons release parameters. As the computer signalled the bombs to leave the aircraft, the jet would turn onto its escape heading and the radar would be turned to air-to-air mode to sanitise the area ahead. The newness of LANTIRN, meant that few of the AAQ-14 targeting pods were available. Strike Eagle crews therefore relied on their radar picture when visual identification of the target was not possible. AUTO bombing mode would be selected by the crew, and the pilot would concentrate on 'flying' radar-driven steering commands in his HUD in order to put the jet in the right part of the sky for the bombs to hit their target. Attacking the 'Scud' sites was a risky business, as they were always well

defended. In daylight deliveries, the F-15E would often AUTO-TOSS its unguided munitions onto the target. This delivery required the pilot to roll the aircraft inverted from 9144 m (30,000 ft), and point the nose towards the target. With wings rolled level, once the small pipper in the HUD passed over the target he would depress his pickle button (on the control stick). This action told the radar 'this is where I want the bombs to hit', and with this accomplished, the pilot would then pull back on the stick and 'loft' the bombs at the target – the computer would decide the best point in the manoeuvre at which to release the bombs. In such deliveries, it was common practice for the crews to fly no lower than 4572 m (15,000 ft), lest they enter the deadly envelope of the Iraqi's numerous anti-aircraft artillery (AAA) pieces.

With the fixed 'Scud' sites now taken out of action, the hunt moved on to finding and attacking mobile 'Scud' launchers. The mobile launchers were responsible for making up to eight launches a night, and were continuing to harass Israel. Unbeknownst to the USAF at the time, the Iraqis were hiding their mobile 'Scuds' in specially adapted buses and underneath road bridges; they were inventive and highly skilled in the art of deception and camouflage. The Northrop Grumman E-8 J-STARS (Joint Surveillance Target Attack Radar System) had

The F-15E was so new that very few of the weapons available in the armoury were cleared to be used by the aircraft. Ordinarily Edwards AFB would test different weapons loadings and carry out very controlled test flights to ensure that the weapon did not contact the aircraft upon release – such a test is seen in the accompanying picture of an 'ED' tail-coded F-15E conducting tests with Mk 84 LDGP bombs. Through necessity, F-15E crews in *Desert Storm* often decided upon their own bespoke weapons configurations, and dropped munitions that had not been cleared for carriage. (Paul F. Crickmore via Steve Davies)

prematurely finished its own OT&E programme and had been rushed to the region. It carried a massive SAR and ground moving target (GMT) radar in a canoe under its lower fuselage, and was able to see many, many miles into Iraq and Kuwait. TACC in Riyadh assigned F-15Es and A-10s to work 'Scud' boxes (patches of desert where 'Scud' launches might be possible) every night with the E-8. If a suspected 'Scud' was picked up on radar, the E-8 would pass the coordinates and the striker would put the bombs on the target. The E-8 was so new that there was no established procedure for co-ordinating with it, but crews persevered and learned to work well together. The F-15Es would patrol their 'Scud' box for four to six hours, after which they would be relieved by another flight, and would then move on to drop their ordnance on secondary targets – anything from armour to artillery pieces.

The F-15E was an astounding success, despite some of the disadvantages facing its crews (limited experience in the aircraft, lack of

approved weapons loadouts as a result of limited testing for some weapons, limited numbers of LANTIRN target pods, etc.). Only two jets were lost in combat – F-15E 88-1689 was crewed by Maj. Tom Koritz (pilot) and Maj. Donny Holland, and is thought to have been struck by AAA while attacking a heavily-defended target in the vicinity of Basrah on 18 January. Neither crewmember attempted ejection. F-15E 88-1692 was struck on the left side by an SA-2 following multiple missile launches from a target complex some 8 nm (15 km; 9 miles) away. Col David Eberley (pilot) and Maj. Tom Griffin ejected, were captured, and spent the rest of the war as POWs. That the losses to the Strike Eagle community were as low as two, is testimony to both the professionalism and competency of the aircrew (many of whom were fired at on their first ever combat sortie), as well as to the capabilities of the jet itself. It also bore witness (as did the staggeringly low losses throughout the whole air war) to the lessons learned and effectively implemented following the Vietnam War. Regular deployments, realistic training exercises such as *Red Flag*, and attention to detail had paid off.

14 February 1991, is a significant date in the history of the F-15E Eagle. On this day, it scored its first and only air-to-air kill – against an Mi-24 'Hind' helicopter. In response to a request for help from US Special Forces (SF), AWACS had called Capt. Richard T. Bennett and Capt. Daniel B. Bakke's F-15E to ask for assistance. Arming and selecting a single GBU-10 LGB, Bennett took the F-15E at mil power through bad weather and into the area as directed by AWACS. At 50 miles (80 km) out, Bakke picked up contacts on his radar. As his jet broke through the weather at 914 m (3,000 ft), Bakke picked up the targets on the TP (cued by the radar). The F-15E closed the last 32 km (20 miles) to the contacts as Iraqi AAA crews fired their weapons towards where they thought the F-15E was. With two of the three helicopters now clearly visible in the Target Pod (TP), Bakke pickled the GBU-10 9.6 km (6 miles) from the target – it would have had a 30-second time of flight to reach the 'Hind'. As the 30 seconds came and went, the crew began to believe that the bomb had missed and failed to detonate. Bennett pulled the jet into a left turn – he was going to come back and target the helicopters with an AIM-9 or two. But as he

From 1993, the 48th FW, RAF Lakenheath, provided F-15Es from its resident squadrons (492nd and 494th FSs) in addition to F-15Cs (493rd FS) to support ongoing operations in the Balkans theatre. F-15Es proved themselves to be the only platform upon which NATO could depend during times of inclement weather and reduced visibility. Although sometimes controversial, the conflicts provided the USAF with a valuable opportunity to test the F-15E once again. (Steve Davies)

reefed the jet around, the 'Hind' blew up and literally vapourised. The SF troops on the ground had estimated the helicopter to be at about 245 m (800 ft) when the bomb impacted just in front of the main rotor. A call, 'COUGAR [AWACS], PACKARD FOUR-ONE [F-15E], splash one helicopter [one helicopter shot down]', was duly made. Bakke and Bennett continued, amid much confusion caused by an incompetent AWACS controller, to target the second 'Hind'. Despite reacquiring the Mi-24 on radar, fuel considerations and a real concern that they might kill a friendly SF helicopter forced them to return to base. The pair had just made history, but it would not be officially recognised until 2 November 2001, when the USAF painted a green kill marking on the side of jet '487.

The Balkans

Following the official cessation of Operation *Desert Storm*, the Coalition nations continue their presence in Turkey and Kuwait in order to patrol the Iraqi No Fly Zones. F-15E and F-15C aircraft are a key part of this, and continue to rotate in and out of three-month AEF deployments at the time of writing (these are known as Operation *Northern Watch* and Operation *Southern Watch*). In the years that followed 1991 however, other trouble spots around the world were soon to become the new focus of attention.

From 1993 onwards, F-15s from several USAF and USAFE wings deployed to Aviano AB, Italy to provide support for a range of operations. By July 1993, F-15Cs from Bitburg's 53rd FS had flown over 660 CAP sorties to protect NATO troops on the ground in the regions of Banja Luca and Sarajevo. Later that year, eight F-15Es from the 492nd FS deployed to Aviano as part of Operation *Deny Flight*. Along with some of aircraft from its sister squadron, the 494th FS, the 492nd remained in Italy for more than a year. When matters worsened in November 1994, NATO commanded a limited strike against Serbian targets in Croatia, in particular Udbina airfield. Eight 492nd Strike Eagles took aloft GBU-12s as part of a 30-aircraft strike package. Their targets were the destruction of SA-6 surface-to-air missile (SAM) sites, although the sortie was cancelled in mid-air the flight was unable to persecute the attack due to stringent ROEs. Once again, Lakenheath's F-15Es were

launched in December, this time to destroy a pair of SA-2 SAM sites which had recently fired upon two Royal Navy BAe Sea Harriers. Operation *Deliberate Force* was started in August 1995, following the mortar shelling of a market square in Sarajevo. Five punitive strikes hit Serbian armour and supplies around Sarajevo on 30 August. A day later, three more strikes were flown. GBU-10s and GBU-12s were dropped by 'LN' F-15Es on 5 September, as the strikes became more widespread. Four days later, the GBU-15 was dropped for the very first time in anger by the F-15E – nine were used to strike air-defence targets around Banja Luca.

In 1998, Operation *Allied Force* was launched. Following repeated NATO warnings to President Milosevic to remove his armed forces from Kosovo, 15 F-15Cs from the 493rd FS, 48th FW were deployed to Aviano. With the deployment came a revision of the force structure being operated in the Balkans theatre (the Airborne Expeditionary Wings were devised). A five-phase plan was put into effect – initially the NATO flights would act as a deterrent; becoming more aggressive if NATO's demands were not met. Despite some gains made at the Rambouillet talks in France, an additional 12 F-15Es from the 492nd FS were sent to Italy in February 1999.

As F-117 'Stealth Fighters' arrived at Aviano AB, the F-15Cs from Lakenheath were displaced to Cervia AB, while being reinforced to a total strength of 18 aircraft. Six 494th FS F-15Es had arrived in December 1998 to allow the 492nd FS's jets to leave for Turkey – they had been committed to Operation *Northern Watch*.

Operation *Noble Anvil* was the name given to the US portion of *Allied Force*. *Noble Anvil* commenced on the night of 24 March 1999. Following several conventional air-launched cruise missile (CALCM) strikes by B-52s, the 26 F-15Es in-theatre, concentrated on striking air defence (SAM, AAA, GCI and early warning) assets, as they followed behind a wall of Lakenheath F-15Cs flying offensive counter air (OCA) sorties. As the conflict progressed, the 'Mud Hen' crews turned their hand to dropping CBUs (cluster bomb units) and other types of weapon. The GBU-28, which is a bunker-penetrating laser-guided bomb, was used once during *Noble Anvil*. Originally developed for

The AGM-130 is a powered, stand-off version of the GBU-15. The GBU-15 is a 2,000-lb (907-kg) precision-guided munition which features large aerofoils to permit long glide distances in addition to an IR or electro-optical seeker head which allows the WSO to steer the bomb onto the target visually. The AGM-130 adds a solid rocket motor to extend stand-off range to beyond that of most SAM systems. GPS was installed in 1995, making the weapon capable of guiding itself to the target area without user intervention, although in nearly all cases the WSO would steer the weapon onto the target manually. (Boeing)

F-111F crews during Operation *Desert Storm*, the GBU-28 can penetrate 30 m (100 ft) of concrete before exploding. It was used against an underground hangar at Prisitna AB, although the attack would appear not to have been successful. The powered version of the GBU-15, the AGM-130, was also used during Operation *Allied Force*. Initially used without success in Iraq that same year, the AGM-130 was used to destroy two MiG-29s on the ground.

The 493rd FS claimed four MiG-29s destroyed during the *Allied Force*. Two were killed on the opening night of the war, when Capt. Mike Shower fired an AIM-120 at a MiG-29 lifting off from its airfield at Batajnica. The other fell to Lt. Col Caesar Rodriguez, who already had three kills to his name from Operation *Desert Storm*. Shower had initially fired two advanced

Following the terrorist attacks on New York in September 2001, the F-15 has been heavily engaged in the US-led war on terrorism. Here F-15Es of the 332nd Air Expeditionary Group are rearmed and serviced at their Middle Eastern forward base, prior to resuming strikes against Afghanistan during Operation *Enduring Freedom*. (USAF)

Although the combat operations performed by F-15s over Afghanistan have been prominent, the F-15 has also taken on the round-the-clock air defence of US cities alongside the F-16. Operation *Noble Eagle* continued into 2002 and has seen fully-armed USAF fighters flying CAPs over major conurbations. A 27th FS F-15C from Langley AFB is pictured above over the Pentagon on just such a CAP. The F-15E shown below was tanking before carrying on to deliver a load of LGBs against an Al-Qaeda target. (Both USAF)

medium-range air-to-air missiles (AMRAAMs) without success at the MiG-29, the third, fired at closer range (6 nm (11 km; 7 miles)), had found its target. Rodriguez claimed his fourth kill while flying OCA over Pristina. His kill also involved use of the AIM-120, albeit with the engagement starting and finishing while still BVR.

The final two kills for the 493rd FS came courtesy of Capt. Jeff Hwang on 26 March 1999. Hwang was flying a defensive counter air (DCA) sortie over Bosnia when AWACS called out two MiG-29s flying into Bosnian airspace. The MiGs were soon picked up on radar by Hwang and his wingman. As the 'Fulcrums' changed direction and started on an intercept course for Hwang's flight (DIRK), Hwang sought permission to fire, following IFF and radar indications that the contacts were indeed hostile. AWACS was slow to respond, and as the MiGs broke 48-km (30-mile) separation, Hwang made the decision that ROE had been met and that he was absolutely confident that his cockpit indications of a hostile target could be trusted. Initially it was Hwang's wingman who fired – Lt 'Boomer' McMurray – but moments later Hwang fired two AIM-120s as well. Despite the F-15s closing to visual range, two of the AMRAAMs hit home. Both kills were later attributed to Capt. Hwang.

4. Accomplishments

Towards the middle of the F-X programme the air-to-ground capability of this new fighter was seen to be at the lower end of the list of priorities – the air-to-air requirement took precedent. The F-X was to be a pure fighter aircraft capable of defeating the numerically superior Warsaw Pact, should it decide to wage conventional, or even nuclear war. To do this, McAir had to look very closely at the problems that plagued the jet that the F-15 would eventually replace, the F-4 Phantom II. A change in political, tactical and strategic thinking within Congress and the USAF played its hand too.

The F-15 was built for speed and manoeuvrability, its clean, aesthetically pleasing lines did little to betray the impressive potential for air-to-ground weapons hauling that it possessed. The F-X programme had initially been a tussle between what Congress wanted for its money and what the USAF wanted to fly – in 1992 the Air Force had the last laugh; its F-15A/C squadrons finally officially closed the book on their air-to-ground training commitments. Only a few wings had ever actively trained in both air and ground capacities, but the entry into service of the ground-attack F-15E Eagle meant that this was a thing of the past. After almost 20 years, the F-15 could now honestly claim 'not a pound for air-to-ground!' (Ted Carlson via Steve Davies and (inset) USAF)

The F-15 marked not only a leap forward in technology, but also a leap forward in the way that the US government actually went about procuring aircraft. Previously, Congress had demanded that the USN and USAF co-ordinate with each other to design, build and procure aircraft that went as far as possible to meet their own individual criteria. This made good short-term financial sense. Despite the exceptionally large budgets allocated to each of the US armed services, it ensured that project and purchase costs were kept low by virtue of bulk buying and close attention to project detail.

Historically at least, this concept had worked in some instances. The US Navy had been the driving force behind the development of McAir's F-4 Phantom, but the USAF had also purchased it once it became apparent that the F-4 could also work well for it. The downside to this philosophy though, was that the compromises that each service had to make in order to accommodate the other often led to the final outcome being a mediocre product. The Navy needed aircraft with enormous power and rapid throttle response, the Air Force had long runways where less stringent safety requirements meant that excess power was less important; US Navy carrier aircraft needed strong, heavy and highly engineered undercarriage and arrester hook installations to allow aircraft to land back on deck in what amounted to no more than a controlled crash, the Air Force used its long runways to float its aircraft down and grease the touchdown. Such fundamental differences in requirements played a major part in the death of the joint USN/USAF effort to develop the F-X, although engine problems with the USN's version of the F100-PW-100 were the final cause for the Navy to eventually pull the plug altogether.

With the USAF looking like the sole domestic F-15 customer, a *carte blanche* presented itself and was quickly exploited. As already discussed, the F-15 was an airframe designed from the outset with the experience of Vietnam in mind. The USAF had lost almost 1,000 aircraft during the war in South East Asia, while many of these losses could not have been avoided, some provided useful lessons for future generations of aircraft designers. The F-4 lacked decent visibility for the crew. The canopy rails extended high up and were above shoulder level, the rail itself was

thick and obtrusive, the forward canopy had two retainer plates right in front of the pilot. These plates held in a thick piece of glass designed to take a bird strike or small-arms fire, but they also blocked some of the forward view out of the cockpit. Rearward visibility for the pilot was also limited, and the WSO could only see above and behind the aircraft, not directly behind it – the ideal perching point for an enemy fighter. McAir came up with a canopy design that fixed these problems in one fell swoop. The forward part of the canopy was constructed of a convex, single piece of reinforced Perspex. This allowed almost unlimited visibility in front of the aircraft. The main canopy hinged several feet behind the pilot and was once again made from a single Perspex moulding. It too bulged outwards (a feature that was to become known as the 'bubble canopy', reusing a term first coined in World War Two). Its ledge rested below the pilot's shoulder level, affording a 360° panoramic view and the ability to look slightly down and to the sides, below the aircraft. With the aid of this convex shape, the pilot could now check both his rear quarter and slightly down to either side of the aircraft without having to command the aircraft to roll or pitch – a common trait amongst F-4 converts, whose 'muscle memory' instinctively drove them to constantly roll left or right in order to see the ground below or to either side. Coupled with HOTAS, the HUD allowed a pilot to make maximum use of this new-found visibility, scanning the skies ahead, to the side and behind for threats and other air traffic. 'It was a real sensation, there was so much you could see, we could turn around and look behind at the tails. In the F-4 and F-106 we couldn't see that well behind us,' said Granrud.

Clarence 'Lucky' Anderegg is another combat veteran of the Vietnam air war. 'Lucky' flew the F-4C/D/E/G, RF-4C and F-15A/B/C/D/E, amassing 2,600 hours in the F-4 and 1,600 hours in the F-15. In addition to this, his logbook shows 365 combat hours in the F-4D. He summed up the differences between the F-4 and F-15 like this, 'The faults corrected between the F-4 and the F-15 are far too numerous to mention. Most notable though, are that the F-4 would go out of control at the drop of a hat. I was never, ever out of control in the F-15 thanks to computerised flight control system, opposable horizontal stabilators and big twin rudders; the HUD; the simple switches all on stick and throttles; the power to burn and finally, the bubble canopy.'

The heart and soul of the F-15 is found at the sharp end of the aircraft. The APG-63 , APG-70 and APG-63(V)I radars are, without question, the single most important facets of the F-15 series. During the 1950s, when many of the fighters that played a role in the Vietnam conflict had been designed, radar was an unwieldy and, as yet, an underestimated technology. At that time radars were extremely heavy, bulky, unreliable, limited in functionality, difficult to use and interpret and required an additional 2.7 kg (6 lb) of aircraft weight for every 0.5 kg (1 lb) of equipment carried. But as technology made rapid advances, processing power increased, component size decreased and so too did weight. Hughes led the race to take these advances and translate them into practical gains.

Whether examining the success of the IDF/AF, or studying the kills achieved during Operation *Desert Storm*, one of the single constants in many cases is that initial acquisition of the target on radar allowed the pilot to manoeuvre into position to make the kill. Be this by firing and guiding a radar-guided missile BVR, or by pressing home the attack by closing to visual range and then unleashing an infra-red guided missile. Hughes had developed a radar and integrated computing systems that would not only automatically tune their performance to suit the required mode as selected by the pilot , but would then interpret the energy bounced back, and display this as readily-digestible information on a radar 'B-Scope'. Later versions of the APG-63 featured advanced radar modes and 'special radar modes'. Much of the detail remains classified, but these radars featured EID and electronic counter countermeasures (ECCM) modes designed to operate when the enemy was attempting to jam the radio frequency (RF) spectrum. Processing improvements allowed radar designers to use the Doppler shift to facilitate a true 'look-down, shoot-down' capability – the radar could intercept low flying targets more reliably than had previously been possible. Instead of a 'swamped' radar display full of false targets, the operator would now see the real target, since 'ground clutter' was rejected. The APG-63 was built with both BVR and WVR

This photograph vividly depicts the enhanced view provided by the F-15's slightly bulbous canopy. Fighter pilots are famous for their sayings, but one,'lose sight, lose fight', has rung true for decades. Even with the modernisation of air combat, engagements continue to occur within visual ranges (as was demonstrated in Operation *Allied Force*). The F-15's canopy features 'Lock' and 'Shoot' lights – these illuminate to advise the pilot that the radar has locked the target and that the missile is ready to shoot – which allows him/her to remain 'heads up' for as much of the engagement as possible. (USAF)

engagements in mind, and while the radar excelled at guiding SARH to their targets at long distances, it was also very capable of scanning the sky ahead at short ranges. Auto Acquisition (AUTO-ACQ) modes allowed the pilot to quickly point the antenna at any patch of sky (within the limits of the radar's gimbals) where he suspected a target might be located. Any target found within 10 nm (18.5 km; 11.5 miles) would then be locked up by the radar and steering cues to the target presented in the HUD.

The APG-63 used a B-Scope radar display in place of the A-Scope used up until that time. B-Scope was the name given to the format in which data was presented to the pilot – looking directly at the screen, the pilot had a bird's-eye view of the radar picture. For example, if the radar was scanning for targets up to 60 miles (97 km) away, any target displayed at the top of the scope was 60 miles distant, or thereabouts. A target 35 miles (56 km) away would be located somewhere just above the middle of the screen; a target 20 miles (32 km) away would appear towards the bottom of the screen, etc. In Velocity-Search mode (used to display those targets with high or slow closure rates), radar contacts that were closing on (moving toward) the F-15 would appear as small arrows towards the bottom of the scope, those going away, as small arrows pointing towards the top. In other radar modes, these would be replaced by small rectangles to which were attached 'velocity vector lines'. These 'vector sticks' as aircrew knew them, would vary in length, depending upon the velocity the target was flying at, and could rotate around their rectangular base to allow the pilot to rapidly identify which direction the target was travelling in (what its heading was). In other modes, the pilot could position a cursor over a target of interest and the radar would instantly display the target's height, airspeed, heading and aspect angle. The APG-63 could monitor, track and engage more than one target simultaneously (provided that the weapons had the capability –

the AIM-7, for example, did not), and this made multi-bogey engagements against a numerically superior force a more realistic option than it may previously have been.

The APG-70 and APG-63(V)I are upgraded versions of the APG-63. They have better memory capability and a Very High Speed Integrated Central Computer (VHSIC), which processes raw radar returns quickly and translates them into digestible data for the pilot. In addition, these radars feature better Raid-Assessment modes, and can better discriminate between closely-formating targets. They also benefit from added sophistication in their handling of ECM. The system reconfigures the radar scan to counter any electronic interference. Specifically, however, they are tailored to work well with the AIM-120 – a missile that needs only limited guidance to the target and for only a small period of time. In theory at least, AMRAAM makes eight simultaneous launches against eight individual targets possible from a single F-15. These features were a first for a fighter aircraft (with the notable exception of the F-14's AWG-9/

The APG-63(V)I/(V)2 and APG-70 feature full AIM-120 compatibility, and are able to ripple-fire the missile against multiple targets. In addition to their excellent long-range capabilities though, they also feature highly useful close-range modes for cueing the AIM-9 Sidewinder missile (pictured here). The AIM-9 itself is a flexible missile which offers a variety of user-selected modes of operation. (Steve Davies)

AIM-54 radar/weapons system) and set the bench mark for future radar developments.

Garth Granrud said, 'The APG-63 was a real revelation. When we locked up a target we now had all this information which previously had not been available to us: speed, altitude, heading, closure velocity, etc. In the F-106 I'd have had to have figured this all out in my head, based on raw data appearing on my radar scope. Now that we have 'vector sticks' and such, it is pretty easy [radar interpretation]. Prior to the APG-63 I had to manually tune my radar or it was useless, it would not discriminate between a large flock of birds, a thunder cell or a contact; I had to do that myself. Now we have multiple target track, etc.' On the evolution of the F-15 radar, he said, 'The differences between the three radars really lie in detection range, tracking capability, low altitude tracking and performance changes in electronic countermeasures environments. Each radar had growing pains as it was introduced to service; we couldn't pick up targets at a certain range or altitude combination for example, but the engineers fixed those problems fairly quickly.'

More recently, the USAF added another piece of hardware to supplement the capabilities of the F-15 – Fighter Data Link (FDL). Tactical aviators rely on situational awareness in combat, without it they could have the world's best equipment but might still fail against a lesser-equipped adversary. Situational awareness is a real-time, mental picture built up by aircrew, and used to make educated decisions about the placement of their aircraft, the tactics they will adopt and the way in which they will derive maximum effect from their weapons systems. During the Vietnam War, US pilots and WSOs would rely on external agencies such as *Red Crown*, the US Navy's radar ship, to tell them where other friendly fighters were, where enemy MiGs were and what their intentions seemed to be. Much pre-mission planning and thoroughness during briefings gave aircrew some idea of what to expect, but once airborne, their own in-cockpit data was limited, making decisions on a tactical level a much more difficult proposition. This often resulted in missed opportunities, and sometimes, in losses. The only data sharing possible happened over the radio, and this was frequently jammed by the beeping of emergency locator beacons or the fast-paced chatter of other flights ingressing or egressing their targets. Elaborate plans such as Operation *Bolo* were drawn up by pioneering USAF aircrew to take advantage of the same weaknesses that faced the enemy, but successes like this were infrequent.

Granrud recalled that in certain areas, the concept of FDL or the similar Joint Tactical Information Distribution System (JTIDS) was not new, 'In the F-106 we had a 'LINK-16' system with full ground control info – a sophisticated system at that time which eventually fell out of favour – we could make an intercept with it without ever even turning our radar on'. But this technology had been developed to allow ground controllers with very powerful, long-range radars to take control of a fighter with a much smaller radar-detection range, and guide it into position, not so that fighters could share data.

Similar in concept to the Joint Tactical Information Distribution System, FDL works by taking the information from the sensors in FDL-equipped aircraft and then sharing that information with similarly-equipped aircraft in the local vicinity (which could be as far or near as was required). Tested by the USAF and ANG in 1997 and then operationally in 1999, the system was deemed to be 'operationally effective and suitable'. Full rate production of FDL was confirmed for FY2000, and 617 units were ordered at a total programme cost of $180 million. FDL was installed in both C- and E-model Eagles, and consists of a modular set of hardware, the Multifunction Information Distribution System-Low Volume Terminal (MIDS-LVT), an FDL terminal, a remote power supply and supporting F-15 cockpit displays and controls. It works by allowing the F-15's radar to digitally pass information on contacts to the FDL unit, which then encrypts it and transmits it to other aircraft via LINK-16. These aircraft can, in turn, distribute this back to other FDL-equipped machines. Meanwhile, the same aircraft is fed information on what other friendlies are seeing in real time. In the cockpit, the Multi-Purpose Display (MPD) shows a bird's-eye view image of the airspace and battlefield in front, to the sides and behind the aircraft.

Fusing the data from a range of other aircrafts' sensors, including AWACS and J-STARS, is accomplished using LINK-16; a robust, high-data, digital link used by many joint US

Fighter data link is the avionics 'toy of the day' in F-15 circles. It will allow secure data transfer between types fitted with the necessary software and hardware, and will revolutionise the way in which future wars are fought. While it may not solve all of the problems associated with the 'fog of war', it may diminish the possibility of 'blue-on-blue' friendly-fire incidents, while increasing the effectiveness and efficiency with which the enemy is vanquished. The F-16, pictured right, is also slated to receive FDL. (Ted Carlson)

reconnaissance and intelligence gathering platforms. By virtue of its ground-attack capability, the F-15E enjoys additional advantages when using FDL. Ground targets can be displayed and uploaded from J-STARS. This information can then allow precise targeting without the need to broadcast tell-tale radar emissions until the very last minute, if at all. The F-15E's highly accurate embedded GPS/INS can guide the crew to the target(s) uploaded by J-STARS (or any other FDL platform) with pin-point accuracy, even if these targets are not immediately visible on radar or to the eyes of the crew. FDL creates a tremendous amount of situational awareness for the crew, without the need to even turn their own radar on. It means new tactics can be created that capitalise on stealthy, multi-directional, co-ordinated attacks.

Survivability

Systems redundancy is a term heard frequently today. The concept behind redundancy is to provide more than one set of systems to power an aircraft's functions. Vietnam had once again been the proving ground for this aspect of aircraft design – many losses resulted from combat damage and general systems failures that today might go unnoticed. The F-105 was a good example of how an aircraft had been built with either a single set of systems, or two sets placed closely together. Hydraulic lines that carried hydraulic fluid to power the massive horizontal stabilators, were too closely arranged in the F-105, they also lacked any form of protection from enemy fire. The stabilisers were critical to flight, as they caused the aircraft to climb or descend as per the pilot's inputs on the control stick. Total loss of hydraulic pressure would cause these 'stabs' to fail, which meant that they would abruptly, and without warning, revert to their unpowered position; pointed a few degrees above the waterline of the aircraft. Basic aerodynamics meant that a sudden and irreversible pitch down of the nose would occur. This unfortunate event led to the death of many pilots who might otherwise have been able to nurse their jets back over friendly territory to eject, or at worst simply eject immediately. It was a direct result of poor positioning of the F-105's hydraulic systems, which were all closely located, increasing susceptibility to battle damage, and the designers not building in redundancy in the form of electrically driving the stabs to a level or slight nose-up attitude in the event of hydraulic failure. This, and many additional deficiencies in the F-105, F-4, F-104, F-100 and others, led to McAir taking a long hard look at systems redundancy planning.

The F-15 therefore incorporates a myriad of improvements in aircraft safety design. Three individual power control (PC) hydraulic circuits power the aircraft's flight control systems. PC1 and PC2 are the main circuits dedicated to powering the flight controls. The utility system powers all other systems dependant on hydraulic pressure, but also serves as a back-up for PC1 and 2. These individual circuits can further be broken down into two or more smaller sections to provide additional redundancy. Reservoir level sensing valves monitor the 'health' of each system and shut off any system which might be leaking fluid. The F-15 was designed to be able to fly with only one functional system. The air inlets are also hydraulically actuated, but feature an electrical back-up that drives them to the full open position in the event of a failure, thus allowing the engine to ingest enough air to keep the engines running. The ACES II ejection seat offers double, triple and quadruple redundancy in a similar fashion to the hydraulics, with one or more firing mechanism installed to fulfil a single function, and a host of other complicated pyrotechnic improvements.

The F-15's flight control system consists primarily of a complex hydromechanical control system linked directly to the stick, throttle and rudders via rods and pulleys. In addition to this, the control augmentation system (CAS) makes fine adjustments to the aircraft's control surfaces to keep it trimmed and to dampen out any unwanted movement. The CAS computers take pitch, roll and yaw inputs sensed by 'stick force sensors' in the pilot's stick, and translate these into control surface movements. The F-15 was heralded as the first fly-by-wire (FBW) fighter aircraft at its launch, although by today's standards, it would take a rather liberal interpretation of 'FBW' to agree! The advantage CAS offers is that the control characteristics of the jet can be changed in flight to help the pilot manoeuvre the aircraft to its limits. The distinction between the F-15's Automatic Flight Control System (AFCS), and that of a true FBW aircraft (like the F-16) however, is that CAS will not prevent the pilot from exceeding flight-envelope limitations. The Overload Warning System (OWS) was installed during MSIP to enable the pilot to manoeuvre with greater confidence, without overstressing the airframe. It consists of aural tones (and a HUD reference)

McAir's designers had taken heed of the hard lessons learned in South East Asia. This F-15D suffered an hydraulics failure in October 2001, but made an uneventful arrested landing soon afterwards. The existence of three separate hydraulic systems in the F-15 meant that this failure was 'partial' – the failed system was automatically isolated and the remaining two continued to power critical aircraft functions to permit landing. Such a failure in the F-105 might have been more dramatic! Note that the tail hook has been extended. (Steve Davies)

which alert the pilot as the *g* increases. As *g* continues to rise, so the 'beeps' increase in frequency, until a steady tone is heard in the headset – indicating that additional *g* would break the jet. A synthesised female voice barks 'Over G! Over G!' through the earphones in the event that this limit has been exceeded. In the F-15E and MSIP II F-15, the hapless flyer can then consult an OWS screen which tells him (or her) how much *g* has been pulled, and what level of damage might have been caused to the airframe. Anderegg commented that, 'The [F-15's] FCS [Flight Control System] was the first FBW overlay on a hydromechanical system. The CAS monitors and assists, but you can fly without it. New algorithms came out from the B model for the E model. We have an auto trim function to take the weight off the stick. It limits rudder at certain speeds – it locks them out at 1.5M.'

These features of strength, survivability, redundancy and technology all combined to dramatic effect in 1983. An IDF/AF F-15D was flying a practice air-combat sortie against a gaggle of Douglas A-4 Skyhawks, when it collided with one of the A-4s over the Negev

The picture that shocked everybody – this brochure dramatically demonstrates the strength and survivability inherent in the F-15 airframe. Dominating the picture is the IDF/AF F-15D, minus its right wing! The aircraft was sent back to Boeing for repair. Within a few months it was flying again; it downed a Syrian aircraft less than a year after the incident. (Boeing/IDF)

Desert. The A-4 had punched through the imaginary maximum height for the engagement, striking the F-15D (which had climbed out of the mêlée that ensued below it for the very reason of avoiding a collision) and ripping off its entire right wing. With frantic calls on the radio to confirm that the A-4 pilot had ejected and to pinpoint his parachute, the F-15 pilot lost control of his Eagle. Unable to know exactly what the damage to his right wing was (fuel vapour being sucked from the severed wing/fuselage fuel pipes prevented him from seeing where he thought his wing was), he managed to regain control of the aircraft via application of aileron and rudder, re-energising the CAS system (which had tripped during the collision) and some judicious use of afterburner to bring the aircraft up to 270 kt (500 km/h; 311 mph) – the speed at which it just about remained flyable. Finding that none of his warning lights had illuminated, the pilot dialled the coordinates of a nearby air base into the INS, and then followed the steering cues to make a landing. Calling the tower several times, he eventually managed to request that a crash net be erected at the end of the runway and the 'cable' be raised to help arrest his landing. He flew a straight-in approach, having lowered his arrester hook to snatch the cable at the beginning of the runway. The cable was snagged at 280 kt (519 km/h; 322 mph), taking 100 kt (185 km/h; 115 mph) worth of energy from the Eagle, before the arrester hook was ripped away from its mount. Now, at 160 kt (296 km/h; 184 mph), the pilot applied delicate braking as the jet hurtled towards the barrier. Finally, it stopped, only 10 m (33 ft) away from the net. The F-15 pilot reflected, 'We got out of the aircraft completely stunned. I still couldn't comprehend a thing, and a huge, dumb smile was plastered all over my face. We were immediately surrounded by [A-4] pilots from the base…a moment of astonished silence took hold. N was the first to speak. "Tell me" he said, turning to me, "can I swap to the F-15?"'

Surprisingly, there are few pictures of the jet having landed, although McAir was informed of the event while one of its tech reps made a routine visit to the squadron. Having personally seen the jet, minus a wing, he recounted that McAir's own studies had shown that an F-15 needed at least the first two-thirds of its wing in place to remain aerodynamically sound!

5. Variants

The F-15A and B entered service with the 1st TFW, at Langley AFB in January 1976. The A model is the single-seater while the B model is a dual control two-seater used for training and evaluation purposes. There had initially been a designation of TF-15A for the latter variant, although this was dropped in favour of F-15B in October 1978. The F-15A/B was the first jet fighter to achieve 7,300 hours of trouble-free flight before experiencing its first loss. Aircraft 73-0088 was lost following a successful low-altitude ejection on 15 October 1975 as a result of smoke in the cockpit. It would be another two years and 30,000 flight hours on 177 operational F-15s before the second loss occurred (by way of a mid-air collision).

The F-15 enjoyed a relatively trouble-free bedding in period, although the F100 engines had more than their share of teething troubles.

A 1st FW F-15C Eagle launches an AIM-120 at Tyndall AFB's weapons range in Florida. The 1st FW, Langley AFB, Virginia, was the first unit to equip with the F-15A in 1976. (USAF)

These problems stemmed mainly from a tendency for the engine to stall during high-angle-of-attack manoeuvres and due to some overheating problems in the turbine section. Many of these hiccups were ironed out by the development of new materials, maintenance procedures and small modifications to the engine itself.

HUD and HOTAS

F-15A/Bs differed little from test F-15s. They incorporated the refinements made during the course of testing, a revised speed brake and dog tooth indents in the horizontal stabilisers, but were otherwise outwardly very similar. From a pilot's perspective, the operational F-15s differed from the test airframes in that they carried a final avionics suite and cockpit instrumentation not seen before. Most notably, they now featured a HUD in the form of two pieces of glass positioned in front of the pilot's line of sight, onto which flight information and weapons release parameters could be projected. The F-15

was not the first aircraft to feature a HUD (the A-7 Corsair II was), but it was the first fighter to do so. Many pilots who had been selected for the F-15 programme had come from the F-4, F-105, F-100, F-101 and F-102 – aircraft which had utilised a primitive sighting system, but which otherwise compelled the pilot to look down into the cockpit during critical phases of flight (such as take-off, landing, bombing and dogfighting) to check that airspeed, altitude, rate of descent and weapons selection parameters were as required. Central, air data and weapons computers would converse with anything from the radar to the INS to present steering symbology on the HUD, which displayed flight data and guided the pilot to the right place to drop bombs, or the right patch of sky in which to intercept an enemy aircraft. The HUD allowed the pilot to spend more time looking out of the cockpit than previously, and in doing so increased the pilot's spare mental capacity to deal with other tasks.

HOTAS was yet another engineering feat which worked well with the HUD to allow faster and less complicated manipulation of the F-15 and its weapons system. The Vietnam War had once again provided valuable lessons to aircrew and design engineers. Setting up the bombs or missiles in the F-4 had required up to as many as twelve different switch selections. These selections invariably required the pilot to look down into the cockpit to ensure that he was flicking not just the right switches, but the right switches in the right order. Understandably, such a practice is a little impractical in the heat of combat, and led to missed opportunities to shoot down enemy MiGs and destroy targets of opportunity on the ground, but was the best that could be achieved with the technology available at the time.

HOTAS addressed this issue by providing switches on the throttles and control column which instantly commanded the F-15's avionics to enter certain modes, and which armed missiles for immediate launch. The control stick carried buttons which were ergonomically mounted and could therefore be pressed by the pilot's fingers and thumb. These switches performed a range of functions, from uncaging the AIM-9 from the radar, to driving the radar into any of a number of Super-Search/Auto-

Acquisition modes. The throttle was the coup however. It carried finger lifts which dispensed chaff and flares; a rotary dial under the left little finger which drove the radar up and down; a small, round, Target Designator Control button which could be pressed up, down, left or right, to move the cursors on the radar screen; an IFF interrogate switch and a 'boat switch' which forced the weapons computer to set up, arm and energise either the AIM-7, or AIM-9, missiles. Each button and switch had its own shape and feel, allowing pilots to quickly learn what each switch did and where it was positioned. Although it took some time to master, the system was effective and much liked. Modern HOTAS systems have increased in complexity by several orders of magnitude, but this first attempt at HOTAS was an innovation which would have far reaching effects in the future.

Granrud remarks, 'The HUD was great, but guys like me, who'd been trained to fly and fight on instruments, took a while to learn to utilise the HUD properly. New guys nowadays rely heavily on the HUD, they don't like instruments. My tendency was to use the HUD occasionally, but I was keyed more to the instruments. Whilst BVR I spent most of my time head down; checking instruments, radar and RWR, as I had been taught to do. The F-15's HUD is not instrument certified – there is no failure mode – nothing to say 'you have a problem' if things start to go wrong with it. Headings can be off, or altitude and airspeed inaccurate and you would have no idea. The HUD cannot be used for instrument flying, although the new guys fly using it whilst cross-checking with other instruments as part of the instrument cross-check.'

Hughes AN/APG-63 radar

The APG-63 had progressed well during the course of testing and evaluation and represented

Opposite: HOTAS was developed by McAir specifically for the F-15, although previous fighters had incorporated elements of it. This image depicts the functions of the pre-MSIP F-15 control stick – even more complex was the throttle quadrant, which controls weapon selection, radar antenna elevation, target acquisition and selection, AIM-9 seeker head orientation and a host of other functions. (USAF via Steve Davies)

CONTROL STICK
(BEFORE TO 1F-15-1262)

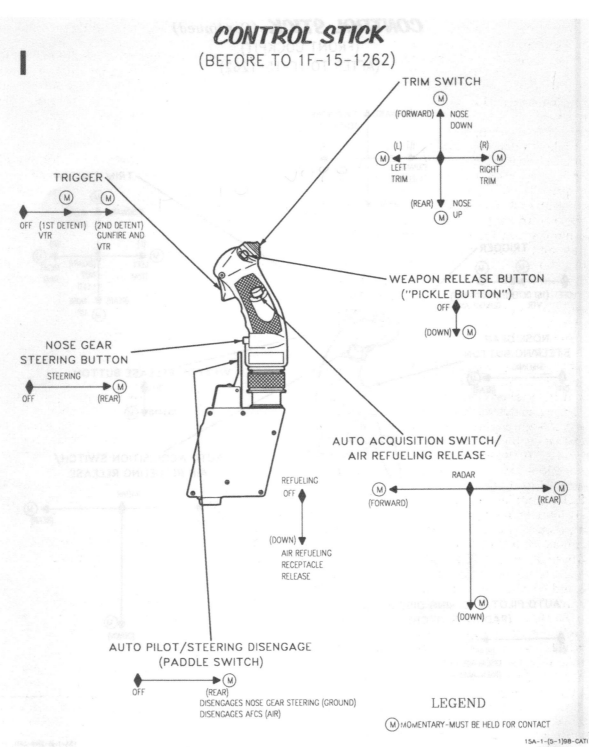

TRIM SWITCH

(FORWARD) — NOSE DOWN

(L) LEFT TRIM — (R) RIGHT TRIM

(REAR) — NOSE UP

TRIGGER

OFF — (1ST DETENT) VTR — (2ND DETENT) GUNFIRE AND VTR

WEAPON RELEASE BUTTON ("PICKLE BUTTON")

OFF — (DOWN)

NOSE GEAR STEERING BUTTON

STEERING — OFF — (REAR)

AUTO ACQUISITION SWITCH/ AIR REFUELING RELEASE

REFUELING OFF — (DOWN) AIR REFUELING RECEPTACLE RELEASE

RADAR — (FORWARD) — (REAR) — (DOWN)

AUTO PILOT/STEERING DISENGAGE (PADDLE SWITCH)

OFF — (REAR) DISENGAGES NOSE GEAR STEERING (GROUND) DISENGAGES AFCS (AIR)

LEGEND

(M) MOMENTARY—MUST BE HELD FOR CONTACT

15A-1-(5-1)98-CATI

a leap ahead for technology at the time. If offered pilots intuitive control, manipulation and interpretation of radar through a well designed scope and a myriad of effective, fuss-free radar modes. It was the very antithesis of the F-4's radar, which displayed what amounted to raw data returns – these required skilled interpretation on the part of the operator. The pilot could now look at the screen, move his radar's area of coverage around with a little control button under his left hand, designate a target, and instantly be told its altitude, airspeed, range, aspect angle and heading. Simultaneously, the HUD would display a small box in the piece

of sky where the target aircraft was to be found. This helped the pilot to get the nose pointed at the target and cued his eyes on where to look to make visual contact. With this, the pilot could formulate his attack plan with greater ease.

The radar modes on offer were crucial in embracing the continued emphasis on BVR fighter engagements. Using a mixture of pulse repetition frequencies (PRFs), the APG-63 could detect targets at long range and at various altitudes. The pilot chose range settings and modes, and the radar automatically switched between high and medium PRFs to pick up the target. The radar was capable of tracking a single

The APG-63 consisted of a range of Line Replaceable Units in addition to the radar antenna itself. It was powered by the aircraft electrical system, and the antenna was driven by aircraft hydraulic pressure. LRUs could be changed on the flight line should the need arise. In this photograph, the top right LRUs have been 'pulled' for maintenance. This 1976 photograph shows avionics bay '3L', where the APG-63's LRUs were housed. (Dennis R. Jenkins via Steve Davies)

target while continuing to scan the sky ahead for other contacts in Track While Search mode (TWS) and would automatically switch to the necessary high PRFs when a Sparrow missile was launched in order to provide the best form of guidance. The APG-63 also featured a little known VI mode. Visual Intercept mode gave the pilot HUD steering cues to position him directly behind (610 m (2,000 ft)) an adversary or radar contact. This mode was useful in that it allowed safer interception of a target in weather. Later versions of the APG-63 (and APG-70) did away with some of the sophistication of this mode.

For dogfighting, the APG-63 came with several Auto-Acquisition modes. These would automatically lock any contact found within 16 km (10 miles), freeing the pilot up to simply point his jet in the direction he believed enemy fighters to be. The AIM-9 was fully integrated into the F-15 and could be slaved to either the radar or allowed to find its own target. Upon finding a target, the HUD would once again display a box to the pilot in order to allow him to determine where the missile was looking.

TEWS

The F-15 had been given a sophisticated electronic warfare (EW) system which exceeded the complexity of any system used in Vietnam. Collectively known as the Tactical Electronic Warfare System, the TEWS comprised of a radar warning receiver (AN/ALR-56), Electronic Warfare Warning System (ALQ-128) and Internal Counter Measures Set (ALQ-135 – deleted on the F-15B because of lack of space). TEWS was internally mounted, provided the pilot with a sophisticated and largely automated warning and countermeasures capability against threat radars (air and ground), and was tied into the chaff and flare dispensers which were flush-mounted one third of the way back behind the engine intakes, on the underside of the aircraft. TEWS would automatically jam or dispense countermeasures based on both data stored in its threat library and what it decided was the highest priority threat to counter. In some instances, TEWS was not fitted at all as the aircraft entered service, due to a shortage of availability. But, elements of the TEWS system were gradually installed to operational aircraft (the ALQ-135 started appearing in 1977, for

example) and then were continually updated. In the mid-1980s TEWS was extensively modernised under MSIP II.

Much of the F-15's avionics took the form of black boxes known as Line Replaceable Units (LRUs). These LRUs could be replaced on the flight line in a matter of minutes and were housed behind access doors placed principally on either side of the nose. Pilots would power up the aircraft's systems (radar, TEWS, INS, flight controls, etc.) and run Built In Test (BIT) checks which automatically ran error checking routines. With a fault identified, the crew chief would be notified and the offending LRU could be 'pulled' and replaced. Similarly, the F100 engines could be changed in under 30 minutes, although this would have to be done in the hangar and would then require a series of checks before the jet could be declared 'Code I' (mission ready). Overall, troubleshooting the F-15 was more simplistic than with the F-4 it was replacing; reduced downtime and maintenance hours proved testament to this. By virtue of the advanced materials used in its construction, its better maintenance and flying qualities, the F-15 was to become the safest USAF fighter ever. By 1995, the F-15 boasted a safety record of only 1.5 major accidents per 100,000 flying hours.

F-15C and D

The F-15C resulted principally from the USAF's desire to increase the aircraft's combat radius but soon matured into a more capable fighter as a result of subsequent avionics upgrades. The first F-15C flew on 26 February 1979 and was visually distinguishable from the A model by the CFTs fitted to either side of the fuselage. It also benefited from three enlarged internal fuel tanks. The CFTs offered an additional 4423 kg (9,750 lb) of fuel capacity. The F-15C was given a new, improved ACES II ejection seat, improvements in the landing gear to cater for a heavier take-off weight, an additional radio (UHF) and strengthened airframe components. The two-seat version, the F-15D, is identical to the C model save for the deleted ALQ-135 and its second cockpit.

Avionics improvements

The APG-63 was given a new Programmable Signals Processor which allowed the radar to

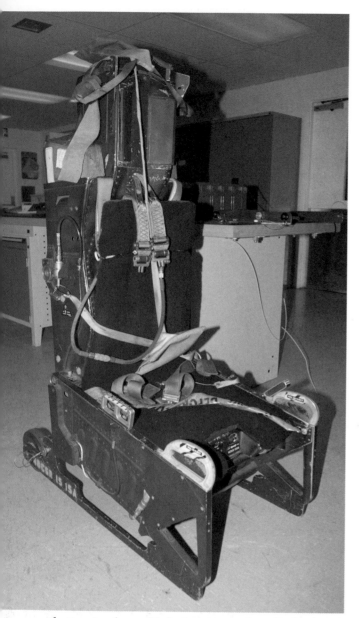

The ACES II ejection seat was manufactured by McDonnell Douglas. It replaced the older Escapac seat on the A- and B-model Eagles. The seat was named Advanced Concept Ejection Seat on account of its improved and expanded ejection envelope. The seat offers a 'zero/zero' capability, meaning that successful ejection can be accomplished while the aircraft is sitting on the ground with no forward airspeed. (Steve Davies)

formation a group of contacts was flying in, or to 'break out' two individual aircraft flying in very tight formation. Armed with this information, the pilot would then have a better idea of the intentions of his foe, and could assign his wingman to engage one while he dealt with the other.

Flying the F-15 aggressively was also made easier with the introduction of the OWS, which resulted in the F-15's placard g limit being raised to 9 g from 7.33 g. The latest version of the ICS – the ALQ-135B – was installed in all C models.

1983, MSIP II arrives

February 1983 saw the introduction of additional modifications to the F-15C fleet. Multiple Stage Improvement Program (MSIP) was a joint venture between McAir and the Air Force Logistics Center. Originally conceived as two programmes to upgrade both F-15A/B and F-15C/D models (MSIP I and MSIP II respectively), the MSIP I component was eventually cancelled as it was deemed to lack cost effectiveness. It was instead decided to implement MSIP II on all F-15Cs rolling off the production line and then to retrofit the entire F-15 inventory, including A models. The first fully upgraded F-15C MSIP II was flown in June 1985 (84-0001)

MSIP II implemented a lengthy list of improvements and modifications to the basic F-15A/C. It created a 25 per cent increase in systems reliability and consisted of installing the Hughes AN/APG-70 radar; upgrading the central computer to make it faster and give it more memory; installing a new Multi Purpose Colour Display (MPCD) to replace the existing armament panel; adding wiring and software to integrate JTIDS; changing the throttles; installing a recording device which could play back images from the HUD and radar screen for mission debriefing and kill validation; improving much

better track multiple targets and to find targets at low altitude – a complicated task as the many radar returns from the ground (often called 'clutter') had caused previous radars great difficulty in identifying target radar returns. Other improvements to the APG-63 included the introduction of a Raid Assessment mode (RAM). RAM could be used to pinpoint a smaller volume of sky and use a fast pre-programmed scan sequence to try and identify what

of the TEWS suite; and adding support for the AIM-120 AMRAAM. Subsequent MSIP II provisions also included the installation of an updated APG-63(V)I radar to replace outmoded APG-63 sets in F-15C/D aircraft. The (V)I version offered similar software and hardware changes to the APG-70, but lacked some of the air-to-ground attack modes.

AESA APG-63(V)2

The USAF purchased 18 (V)2 units in December 1999. The APG-63(V)2 is an improved radar that provides increased pilot situational awareness and takes full advantage of the capabilities of the AIM-120 AMRAAM. The Active Electronically Scanned Array (AESA) radar antenna uses wave manipulation and miniature dipoles to electronically direct the radar beam in the desired scan pattern and direction. The advantages are a reduced number of components necessary to run the radar (hydraulics are no longer needed to steer the antenna dish for example) and a much faster scan pattern. Some sources quote the AESA radar as being able to perform a full scan in two seconds, whereas the APG-63 would take seven or eight. The system also introduced a new and more capable IFF system.

Modified F-15Cs were stationed at Elmendorf AFB, Alaska, from December 2000.

F100-PW-220

Despite the continual improvements and changes made to the PW-100 engine, it still lacked the sophistication and automation necessary to allow the pilot as much confidence in the engine as would have been liked. The afterburning in PW-100 engines often failed to light-off, and the rapid throttle changes necessary in air combat manoeuvring were still causing compressor stalls and stagnation.

Granrud recalled that, 'The F100 had teething problems. Right after it came out, there were difficulties with the engines stalling, stagnating; a perpetual stall. We had an engine control – EEC – which monitored things, but the new DEECs of the -220 and -229 are better than the old, analogue, EEC. If you did things too fast you got into trouble, the EEC couldn't keep up with your control inputs. The P&W guys came around with a team from Boeing and worked out

that it was 50 per cent the operator doing things too fast, and 50 per cent problems with the engines. DEEC was a follow on to make things better. Even now we still have PW-100 engines installed on some A models. The -220 constantly trims the engines and we can use the throttles at will. The F-106 used the J75 or J79 and that was a pretty tough engine; it could take a lot of ice and FOD [foreign object damage]. The blades were pretty thick as we had no dual spool turbine at the front [as on the F100] like today. The engine heralded a quantum leap forward because it produced much greater thrust than had previously been seen, whilst keeping good levels of fuel efficiency. With the F100-PW-100, we had to remember to be careful on requesting AB [afterburner] while we were slow. If you asked too fast you'd get a stall or stag [stagnation]. Guys have gone into stag and not noticed. The master caution light would come on and the generator would drop off-line as you went past 40 per cent engine rpm. One problem we had

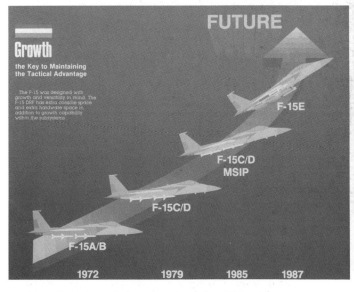

McAir's depiction of the growth of the F-15 airframe. Despite the company's optimism for the 'future', the F-15E and its derivatives were the last major variant produced at the time of writing. The unusual way in which the F-15 has matured means that there can be confusion when identifying F-15 types. Certainly, pre-MSIP II F-15As and Cs looked very much alike, and even MSIP II has done little to alleviate the visual similarities between the variants. (USAF via Steve Davies)

was afterburner burn-though – we eventually solved this by putting in a system to monitor the aft section of the airframe. With an AB burn-through, a flame would attach to the wall of the AB can, it would burn at over 1000°C and you'd have no indication because it was aft of all the other gauges [fire detection systems]. Someone else would tell you you'd have a problem, we'd do a Battle Damage check on him [where the pilot would check the controllability of the aircraft and his wingman would visually inspect the aircraft for damage] and see if there was a hole in the side of the jet. We'd just come out of afterburner to put out a burn-through, sometimes as result of seeing smoke in the mirrors, sometimes because we got a call from

The AESA APG-63(V)2 seen installed on an Alaskan F-15C. The (V)2 offers a much faster scan rate than previous models – it uses an electronically-steered radar beam to detect, acquire and track targets. As a result, the antenna remains static and the hydraulic systems associated with the radar are deleted. This came as a relief to those who had previously had to clean up after the F-15 had suffered a nose bleed! Nose bleeds occurred as a result of ruptured hydraulic lines (which supplied the radar antenna), with pooling of hydraulic fluid inside the radome itself. (USAF)

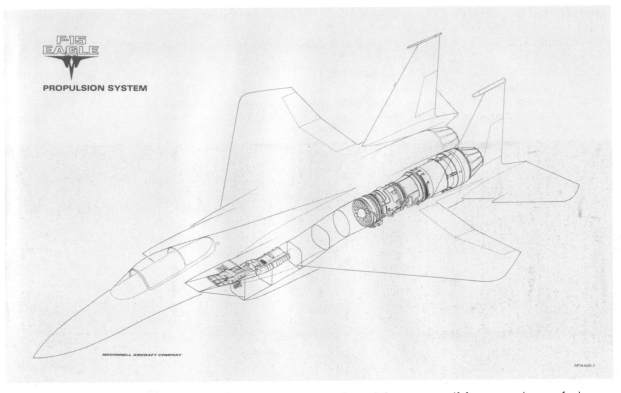

PROPULSION SYSTEM

The engines actually take up very little space inside the aircraft, and the motor itself features a large afterburner section. Hydraulically-driven variable inlet ramps control the speed of the air as it enters the intakes and travels down towards the fan, this assists in smooth engine operation throughout the flight envelope. (Boeing via Steve Davies)

someone else to say "Hey, you're streaming fire or smoke!".'

The F100-PW-100 generates 66.70 kN (15,000 lb st) (105.97 kN/23,830 lb st augmented) at sea level, which was more than enough to push a basic-weight A model to its sea-level limit of Mach 1.23. Given the advances being made in core manufacturing techniques, design of new composites and the microprocessor, a newer version of the engine was developed, the F100-PW-220. The PW-220 offers the same performance as the PW-100, but has the additional advantage of full-authority Digital Electronic Engine Control (DEEC). DEEC serves to reduce wear and tear on engine components while increasing engine performance, decreasing fuel consumption and increasing life span. As one F-15C pilot put it, 'the engine is now smart enough to work out whether the "burner" has lit'. DEEC allows the pilot relatively carefree

operation therefore, although sudden and excessive throttle manipulation is still a matter to which the pilot has to give thought. The PW-220 was installed in limited numbers in late-model F-15Cs, although many US-based F-15 squadrons continue to operate with the PW-100 powerplant.

F-15E/I/S

The F-15E was to prove the ultimate incarnation of the F-15 airframe, and is heralded as the most capable deep-strike fighter in operation at the date of writing. Strike Eagle came about as a result of a combination of clever corporate strategy by McDonnell Douglas, the foresight and vision of TAC commander General Wilbur Creech, and the need to find a replacement for the ageing F-111. Since the inception of the F-X project, the F-15 airframe had had an intrinsic air-to-ground functionality. While this capability had not been used, the F-15A and C were both

An early load of AIM-7 and AIM-9 missiles seen aboard F-15A 72-0113 in June 1975. Early versions of both of the Air Intercept Missiles experienced limited, or at least, disappointing results when used a few years earlier in the skies over Vietnam. Unlike the US Navy's F-14, the F-15 was not ready in time to serve in the South East Asian conflict, although the F-14 arrived too late to actually play a part in hostilities. (Dennis R. Jenkins via Steve Davies)

wired to carry a range of air-to-ground munitions and had basic radar modes to use these stores if necessary. McDonnell Douglas and Hughes had recognised that a two-seat, dedicated-strike version of the F-15 could well be an aircraft that the USAF would show great interest in, and set about developing this concept under the company project name 'Strike Eagle'. This development was something of a gamble as it was financed by company monies and was an unsolicited venture. As it turned out, the consortium received positive encouragement from General Creech, who worried that as the F-111 grew older, TAC would lose its edge in the

deep-strike role – a crucial mission in Western Europe fulfilled by a complement of over 70 F-111Fs and Es divided into two wings (RAF Lakenheath, England and RAF Upper Heyford, England, respectively). With this concern weighing down on him, Creech encouraged McAir to develop its concept. The F-111 was not far from being retired, and in the immediate future would benefit from a stablemate in its role as a nuclear-strike deterrent.

Despite being maligned by the world's media, the F-111F was a potent strike platform that offered long-range, terrain-following and precision-strike capabilities. The Pave Tack pod on the F-111 used infra-red imaging to allow the crew to visually acquire their targets at night. It could also fire a laser onto the target, designating it for laser-guided bombs (LGBs) which home in on the reflected laser energy with pinpoint accuracy. The terrain following radar (TFR) allowed the crew to fly down to 61 m (200 ft) above ground level (AGL) in all weathers, thereby avoiding enemy radar and visual detection.

The Strike Eagle is born

TF-15A (72-0291) was chosen as the Strike Eagle test bed in 1983. Hughes went back to the drawing board with a view to completely overhauling and improving the APG-63 for the air-to-ground mission. The APG-70 was built with a synthetic aperture radar system as standard. This software-driven mode was deleted on the APG-70 fitted to the F-15C, but is at the heart of the F-15E. SAR works by measuring the Doppler shift created when the radar waves hit the ground and bounce back to the radar antenna. Using complex computer algorithms to establish the movement of the aircraft relative to the ground, the APG-70 could interpret this shift and translate it into a picture. The resulting image is a very clear bird's-eye view of the ground, which can be viewed on a display in the rear cockpit. The process through which this is achieved became known as 'patch mapping' and can be achieved down to a resolution of 0.67 nm (1.24 km; 0.77 miles). In addition to SAR, Hughes also refined the Ground Moving Target (GMT) mode in the APG-70. GMT works in the opposite way to SAR – it filters out the returns from the ground, instead concentrating on only those objects which move. GMT can therefore track any moving object on the ground, and is ideal for detecting and targeting objects such as truck or tank convoys.

'291 was initially fitted with CFTs and the AN/AVQ-26 Pave Tack pod from the F-4E and F-111F. The idea was not necessarily to fully integrate this pod into the Strike Eagle – the USAF had already signed a contract with Martin Marietta to produce a lighter-weight, more capable system which was to be christened LANTIRN (Low Altitude Navigation and Targeting by Infra Red at Night), although it is

noteworthy that LANTIRN was actually commissioned for the F-16 and A-10. Prior to testing, '291 underwent a complete rebuild, the airframe was modified to allow a 16,000-hour fatigue life, the forward avionics bays were redesigned (along with changes to the electrical system which supplied them), the space for M61A1 ammunition was reduced as the displaced ALQ-135B electronic black boxes were rehoused, the engine bays were redesigned to allow commonality in plumbing and installation for either P&W or GE engines, and the tail hook was modified to cope with a heavier anticipated landing weight. These modifications permitted a new sustained 9 g capability, but also forced the aircraft designers to install new landing gear and wheels in order to allow the jet to operate safely at higher gross weights. In all, the F-15E weighed in at just under 7257 kg (16,000 lb) heavier than the F-15C (which, after MSIP II, was heavier than the F-15A).

Increased weight and new weapons carriage considerations meant that the PW-220 engine was, for the most part, short of power. P&W had competed in the IPE (Improved Performance Engine) competition against General Electric, and from this came the PW-229, offering a multitude of performance and maintenance advantages over the PW-220. The -229 features an Improved DEEC (IDEEC). IDEEC allows a faster spool time from idle to military power settings, offers 11 stages of augmentation (vs 5 in the -220) and runs with a higher high pressure turbine temperature which, in turn, contributes to an overall increase of just under 26.68 kN (6,000 lb st) in afterburner. The IPE powerplant also reduces maintenance workloads and offers an extended service life. In the air, crews point out that the increase in thrust makes all the difference, and even such things as taxiing require additional attention and focus on account of the high residual thrust provided by the engines. The -229 series of engines first saw service in 1991, but has been installed in only limited numbers. Currently only the F-15Es at Elmendorf AFB and RAF Lakenheath are powered by these motors. Capt. Joe DeFidi, an active service F-15E pilot who first learned to fly the C-model F-15, remarked, 'The first time I jumped into one of these jets [F-15E] with the 2-29s in, I felt like a kid with a new toy – it was a

The F-15E was to be the ultimate deep-strike, precision ground-attack platform. Intended to replace the ageing F-111, it was also destined to fully retain its air-to-air capabilities. Blessed with an even more capable radar than previous F-15 variants, the APG-70, it has proved its worth in a succession of conflicts across the globe. F-15E 87-0183 was the USAF's first production standard Strike Eagle. It is seen here in a promotional brochure with its LANTIRN pod highlighted. (Boeing via Steve Davies)

real kick in the pants. In the C models, we had the -100s. The difference between the two was big; those motors are nice!' Although the F-15E benefited from the additional thrust, it still lacked some of the 'light gray Eagle's' manoeuvrability. Capt. DeFidi continued, 'Because of the extra weight, and the drag from the CFTs you don't get the turn rate you do in the C model. The CFTs are a lot of drag.'

During the course of development, Martin Marietta's LANTIRN was successfully tested and flown, reaching operational status in 1987, although it remained in short supply until well after Operation *Desert Storm* in 1991. LANTIRN consists of two pods mounted on the left and right underside, behind the engine intakes. Designated as the AAQ-13 Navigation Pod and AAQ-14 Target Pod (TP), each is attached via two mounting lugs and simple electrical terminals. The 'Nav Pod' houses a FLIR sensor and TFR and is primarily used by the pilot to allow hands-off low altitude flying in all weather, night or day. The FLIR sensor looked ahead of the aircraft and could display the resulting image onto the pilots' Kaiser, Wide Field of View (WFOV) HUD. The TFR looks ahead and slightly to either side of the jet to detect obstacles and terrain. Mounted on the left pylon is the TP. It is used by the WSO to identify and designate targets when weather conditions permit, and it can be tied to the radar or manipulated independently. It has three selectable fields of view and houses a laser designator. The WSO has to find the target in the TP, put the cross hairs over it and press a button to commit the pod to tracking it. Several tracking options are available, all of which permit the WSO to keep one eye on other systems during the course of the attack run, something that F-111F WSOs were never able to do.

Above and top: LANTIRN consists of two separate pods. The AAQ-13 is mounted on the right of the jet and houses a TFR and the pilot's navigation FLIR system. The AAQ-14 is the Target Pod. It is used to find, track and lase ground targets, as well as to track and cue the radar on to airborne targets. Both pods were originally manufactured by Martin Marietta (now Lockheed Martin), and are remarkably reliable. (Both Steve Davies)

The two-crew cockpit was considerably updated, with an emphasis being placed on interoperability – that is to say, the ability of each crew member to perform almost any function necessary to get the mission done. The front cockpit features two monochrome MPDs and one Multi-Purpose Color Display (MPCD). The rear cockpit houses two MPDs and two MPCDs. An Up Front Controller (UFC) was installed in each cockpit to allow the crew to enter data into the powerful and sophisticated avionics suite.

Lt. Col Clarence 'Lucky' Anderegg, USAF Ret., flew the first operational F-15E sortie. 'Flying the jet [F-15E] was a walk in the park; it was an F-15 and I already had over a thousand

hours in "light grays" – the A and C. Learning the avionics took a little time, especially the Up Front Controller that controls everything, but generally speaking, transitioning to the E was pretty easy. I had many hundreds of hours dropping bombs in the F-4 (I had two tours of duty as an instructor pilot in the F-4 weapons school at Nellis in the '70s) and I knew weapons and weapons deliveries as well as anyone. I thought the E was a joy to fly and was without question the finest machine I ever flew. I mean, it was an order of magnitude better in the air-to-ground role than anything we ever had, including the A-7. It was much better than the F-16, which had short legs [limited range],

The superb interoperability within the F-15E's cockpit cannot be exaggerated. MPCDs and MPDs are clearly seen in this picture of an F-15E front cockpit. Note the radar picture on the left MPD, a bright FLIR display on the right MPD, a digital map on the MPCD (bottom centre), and the Up Front Controller (top centre). Nearly all mission-critical tasks can be accomplished from both front and back seats. (Steve Davies)

small load [of weapons], and a tinker-toy radar! In the air-to-air role, the Strike Eagle was just like a C with CFTs and a moving map display, which is very helpful in air-to-air. The only problem with the jet is that we [the USAF] didn't buy more of them.'

Service introduction
The USAF ordered the F-15E in 1984 having judged it superior in competition with the General Dynamics F-16XL. July 1985 saw McAir fly 86-0183, the first F-15E, for the first time. Two other F-15s (-0184 and -0185) flew soon after. The 33rd TFW at Eglin AFB received the later of the three F-15Es in August 1986 to begin USAF trials, these culminated in the 4th TFW at Seymour Johnson converting from its F-4Es to become the first operational F-15E wing in December 1988. Some 217 F-15Es were built.

F-15I, S and K
Both the I and S airframes are very similar externally to the USAF's F-15E, albeit lacking the ALQ-128 and ALQ-135 fairings and antennas. Internally, there is a marked difference in the avionics suites provided. The US DoD has never approved the export of many of the EW systems incorporated in to F-15E, and the ALQ-128, ALR-56 and ALQ-135 were deleted from export versions. So too were the HAVE QUICK radios and certain other features. Both I and S versions are powered by the PW-229 engine.

The F-15I Ra'am (thunder) is, on paper at least, probably the most capable version of the F-15E in service at the time of writing. The IDF/AF relied heavily on Israel's own highly experienced defence industry to provide jam-resistant radios, EW, Missile Approach Warning System (MAWS), helmet mounted sight (HMS), GPS, central computer and bombing computer equipment for the F-15I. Some 25 Ra'ams were delivered under the FMS designation *Peace Fox*. Martin Marietta supplied 10 TPs to augment the Nav Pods already being used by the IDF/AF F-16 fleet. Despite persistent rumours that the APG-70 fitted to the Ra'am had been 'toned down' to remove some of its more advanced features, it is likely that it retains full air-to-air capability. The air-to-ground High-Resolution Mapping (HRM) mode of the Israeli APG-70 was certainly improved upon, leading to the radar being re-

designated APG-70I. The improvements featured a higher mapping resolution in order to enhance accuracy and locate smaller targets. Integration of GPS saw the all-weather capability of the F-15I increased and protected as a result of additional systems redundancy.

The F-15XP (which became known as the F-15S) was subject to greater deletion of sensitive equipment than the F-15I. Along with the EW equipment, some of the capability of the APG-70 was also downgraded by means of software changes in the associated LRUs. Once again, the radar's designation was changed, this time to APG-70S. The RSAF order was valued at $9 billion, and became the largest US foreign military sale in history. A two-tone Compass Gray paint scheme was adopted for the RSAF Strike Eagle.

A new chapter in the Eagle's history began on 19 April 2002, when Boeing announced that South Korea had chosen the F-15K as the winner of its F-X requirement. Some 40 aircraft are scheduled for delivery between 2005 and 2008. Boeing beat off competition from a number of excellent fighter designs, the final selection choice down to either the F-15K or Dassault's Rafale. The new Eagles will be similarly equipped to the latest USAF F-15Es, with full ARQ-128, ALQ-135 and FDL systems. They will also have the Joint Helmet-Mounted Cueing System (JHMCS) sight, APG-63V(2) radar and the Advanced Digital Cire Processor in place of the standard central computer. Compatibility with the Joint-Direct Attack Munition (JDAM), Surface Land-Attack Missile Expanded Response (SLAM ER) and Wind-Corrected Munitions Dispenser (WCMD) weapons systems will also be provided as, presumably, will supplies of these weapons. Boeing is hopeful that the Republic of Korea's decision to buy Eagles might influence other nations in the region. Most notably, both Australia and Singapore are looking for new fighters and are likely to be targets for marketing from Boeing.

Export fighters
Between the Japan Air Self Defence Force (JASDF), RSAF and IDF/AF, over 400 F-15A/B/C/D airframes were ordered from 1975 onwards. All three forces received very similar aircraft with common features deleted as per the F-15E above.

The F-15's huge wing area, which is similar in size to a tennis court, is evident in this illustration.

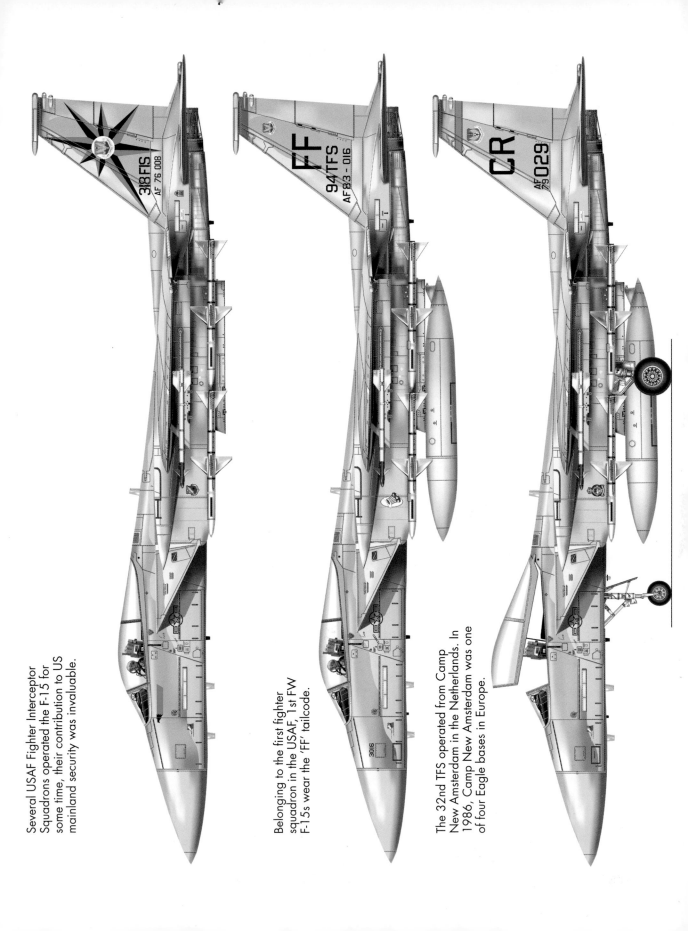

Several USAF Fighter Interceptor
Squadrons operated the F-15 for
some time, their contribution to US
mainland security was invaluable.

Belonging to the first fighter
squadron in the USAF, 1st FW
F-15s wear the 'FF' tailcode.

The 32nd TFS operated from Camp
New Amsterdam in the Netherlands. In
1986, Camp New Amsterdam was one
of four Eagle bases in Europe.

318 FIS
AF 76 008

FF
94 TFS
AF 83 - 016

CR
AF 79 029

The F-15I Ra'am attended the air show at RAF Waddington, UK in June 2001 as part of an IDF/AF contingent. F-15I '291 flew a breathtaking display while carrying a full complement of twelve inert Mk 82 LDGP bombs. Israel's F-15I is very similar to the USAF's F-15E, although it boasts an impressive range of indigenous modifications. (Steve Davies)

Israel was the first export customer, placing an order for 25 F-15As in 1975. A team of 6 IDF/AF pilots had spent time with the USAF evaluating the aircraft as a replacement for Israel's fleet of F-4 Phantoms. The first order paved the way for a total Israeli purchase of 104 F-15s (including the F-15I). Due to production considerations, the first four aircraft to be delivered were from the original F-15 test programme and featured the short speed brake – these aircraft were ferried to Israel in December 1976, and caused a political storm on account of the fact that they had arrived on the Sabbath. Over a year would pass before production-standard F-15A/B aircraft would be delivered to Telnof AB, Israel. Future orders included MSIP II F-15C/Ds, some of which used F-15E airframes as there was a shortage of F-15D airframes. All Israeli F-15s can carry the standard US weapon loads, in addition to the indigenous Shafrir, Rafael Python 2 and Python 4 infra-red guided AAMs and air-to-ground stores. It was the success of AIM-9 and Shafrir missiles which scored the first ever aerial victory of the F-15 on 27 June 1979. A mix of IAF F-15s and Kfirs was flying CAP for a group of IDF/AF bombers, when an Israeli E-2C Hawkeye vectored them towards a flight of Syrian MiG-21s. Despite the Eagles launching a barrage of AIM-7 Sparrows from some distance off, the fight closed to the merge and four of the MiGs were promptly dispatched by the F-15s, leaving the Kfirs to mop up and take credit for a fifth kill. The kill ratio would continue to rise in the coming year or two, with a MiG-25 becoming the twelfth kill in 1981.

December 1977 marked the order of 187 F-15J and two-seat F-15DJs by the JASDF. Following an evaluation of over 12 different aircraft, the F-15J was chosen as Japan's new air superiority fighter to replace the F-4. A licensing agreement was drawn up to allow Mitsubishi, Fuji and Kawasaki to build the vast majority of the airframes locally, thereby providing additional industrial employment and prosperity. As with all FMS F-15s, the F-15J had the ECM and nuclear capability deleted before delivery. Japan, like Israel, has compensated for this by installing its own systems in the empty avionics racks.

Peace Sun was the FMS name for the purchase of 46 F-15C and 16 F-15D airframes by the RSAF. As the most recent customer for the F-15C/D, the RSAF received an initial batch of aircraft on 11 August 1981. The Saudi F-15C differs from that of both Israel and Japan in that it carries the ALQ-135 ICS (earlier orders had this system deleted), but the proximity of Iraqi fighters during Operations *Desert Shield/Storm* in 1991 prompted Congress to approve supply of the system to the RSAF.

Others less familiar

In the 30 years since the F-15 was first produced, several incarnations of this versatile airframe have been noted. Of these, each has its own story to tell.

Streak Eagle (72-0119): This airframe was used for two weeks from 16 January 1975 to establish the capabilities of the F-15 in a controlled and instrumented environment. Three USAF F-15 pilots flew the jet to very precise parameters during this time, thereby achieving several speed and climb world records. The aircraft was heavily modified to reduce weight as much as possible. Among the list of items removed from the aircraft were a generator, the speed brake, flap actuators, utility hydraulic system, non-critical cockpit displays and radios, landing and taxi lights, and radar system. The aircraft was a Cat II airframe, and was already 363 kg (800 lb) lighter than Cat I aircraft prior to any modifications. In all, the jet was reduced to 816 kg (1,800 lb) less than other Block 6 aircraft. The programme cost was $2.1 million.

F-15S/MTD (71-0290): This was a $117.8 million programme awarded to McAir by the USAF in 1984. The total contract cost eventually reached $272 million, and from it was born the F-15 Short Take-Off and Landing/Manoeuvring Technology Demonstrator (F-15S/MTD). The basis for the contract was to test emerging technologies for suitability to the USAF's Advanced Tactical Fighter – the ATF competition being between the YF-23 and YF-22. Controllable foreplanes were added, as were F-15E cockpit switches and layouts, F-15E landing gear, and provision for the APG-70 and LANTIRN pods. Most importantly, however, two-dimensional thrust-vectoring nozzles were added to modified PW-220 engines. These nozzles were made from titanium and carbon fibre, and were able to enhance manoeuvring, take-off and landing performance. They could redirect thrust longitudinally by 20° up and down and could provide full reverse thrust on landing. Finally, they could provide limited amounts of braking thrust while airborne via use of louvres just in front of the divergent/convergent nozzles. Some 350 hours of ground testing was performed by P&W, revealing that the engines and nozzles were capable and relatively trouble free.

To make use of the advanced flying control surfaces and systems, an FBW control system was used to operate the four control channels.

After much political negotiation, and a plethora of options proposed by Boeing, US Congress finally approved the purchase of 72 F-15S aircraft. The RSAF operates two squadrons of the F-15S at the time of writing, and has seen its fleet of Strike Eagles gradually updated by means of US approved software upgrades. (Boeing)

The 48th FW's F-15Es have launched bombing missions direct from their base at RAF Lakenheath, Suffolk, England.

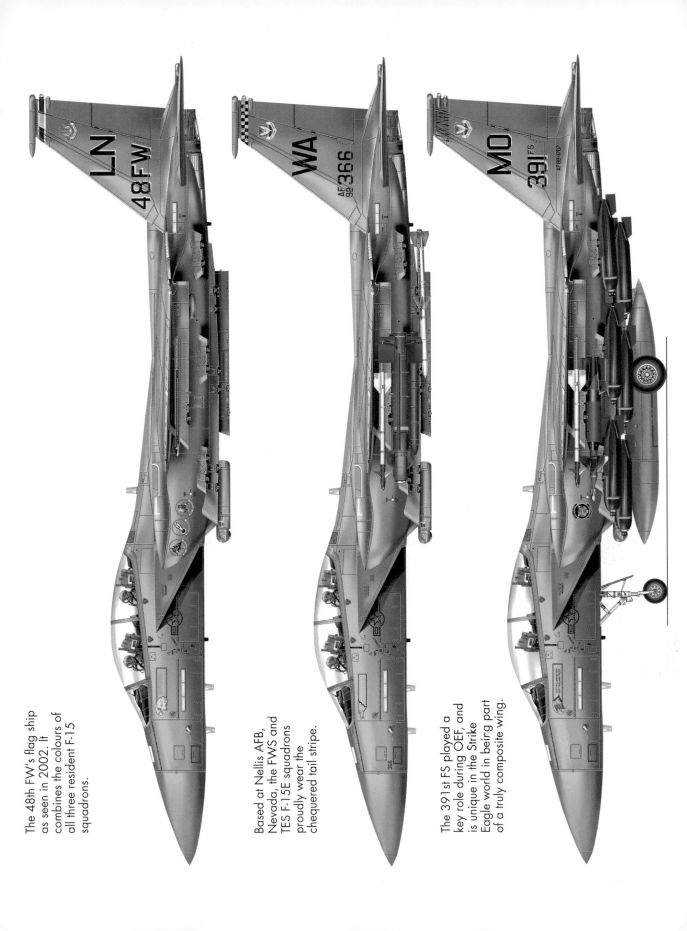

The 48th FW's flag ship as seen in 2002. It combines the colours of all three resident F-15 squadrons.

Based at Nellis AFB, Nevada, the FWS and TES F-15E squadrons proudly wear the chequered tail stripe.

The 391st FS played a key role during OEF, and is unique in the Strike Eagle world in being part of a truly composite wing.

The addition of the foreplanes had expanded the flight envelope of what McAir referred to as the NF-15B, and the jet eventually demonstrated an increased air combat capability in several areas. This included a 50 per cent increase in roll rate, 30 per cent increase in pitch rate, decreased landing rolls, decreased take-off runs and so on. In addition to the raw performance capabilities, interesting technological innovations were also being tested. One such innovation involved using the Nav Pod and APG-70 in concert to provide steering cues to land at an unplanned alternative airfield. The system was demonstrated to allow the aircrew to patch-map an airfield and have the APG-70 automatically provide glide slope steering for a perfect approach. All the while, the pilot referenced the Nav Pod to visually confirm what his computers were telling him. It is unclear if this technology has made its way into the F-22, although the absence of a Nav Pod certainly makes this seem unlikely. The programme ended in 1991, and paved the way for '0291's next testing assignment – ACTIVE.

Advanced Control Technology for Integrated Vehicles (ACTIVE) was a programme started in 1996, based on a similar premise to the S/MTD venture – to test and develop technologies for

An F-15A, armed with AIM-7 and the indigenously produced Python AAM, breaks left in the clear Israeli sky. The F-15B in the foreground is similarly loaded with air-to-air missiles. Israeli F-15s were in combat within 18 months of their acquisition from the US. To date, all of their kills are believed to have been scored against Syrian aircraft. (IDF via Dennis R. Jenkins)

Japan's F-15s are among the most colourful of all. JASDF aggressor squadrons are well known for their more adventurous paint schemes, which serve to both distinguish them from other F-15 operators and to provide a more realistic psychological training environment for their crews. F-15DJ (C-8) 02-8073 is pictured here. (Masahiro Koizumi via Dennis R. Jenkins Collection)

operation use in the next generation of airframes. ACTIVE saw the joint Agencies (NASA, P&W, USAF and McAir) installing a revised thrust-vectoring system onto two PW-229s. Aside from the different engines, the other main difference when compared to the F-15S/MTD was the multi-directional nozzles which could move through +/-20° in any direction (they were known as Pitch/Yaw Balance Beam Nozzles). These Beam Nozzles lacked a braking thrust/thrust reversing capability and could not be vectored at high Mach speed (Mach 2).

NASA

NASA has used a number of F-15s in test roles. 71-0281 was used in December 1975 to test the thermal tiles used by the Shuttle Orbiter. It was handed back to the USAF in 1983, without ever having a NASA designation. 74-0141 was an F-15B used by NASA from 1994 as the Aerodynamic Flight Facility. Numbered as NASA 836, it was used to carry a Flight Test Fixture (FTF) on its centre pylon. The FTF houses systems and materials for testing and instrumentation. A good example of its use was work carried out on the X-33's Thermal Protection System. Equipment installed in FTF II calibrated, monitored and instrumented the materials destined for the X-33, at various

flight velocities, altitudes, temperatures, aerodynamic loadings, etc.

F-15A NASA 835, was acquired on 5 January 1976, and was operated as the Flight Research Facility. Originally 71-0287, it was the eighth production F-15A and has been employed in a variety of guises since then – it is probably the hardest worked of all NASA's F-15s. NASA originally used 835 to test and develop future propulsion systems, aerodynamics, integration, control systems, instrumentation development and flight test techniques (among other things) in 1976. Then, in 1982, it was used to test DEEC for the PW-220 engine. It demonstrated massive performance increases and went on to be the test bed for the F100 IPE. 1986 saw it testing the Advanced DEEC Engine Control System (ADECS); a system used to evaluate and control the stall margin of the engine under different operating parameters. Among the list of results were a decrease in fuel consumption by 15 per cent at constant thrust settings, improved rate of climb by 14 per cent and up to 24 per cent increase in acceleration (the DEEC tests had already demonstrated an increase in acceleration by up to 41 per cent). Most importantly though, no stalls were encountered, not even with the most heavy handed and aggressive use of thrust and manoeuvre.

The Japan Air Self Defence Force
operated a separate squadron of
F-15J and F-15DJ aggressor
aircraft. It was called Hiko
Kyodotai.

The JASDF adopted a complex serial numbering system that incorporated a year of manufacture, aircraft category, role and individual serial number.

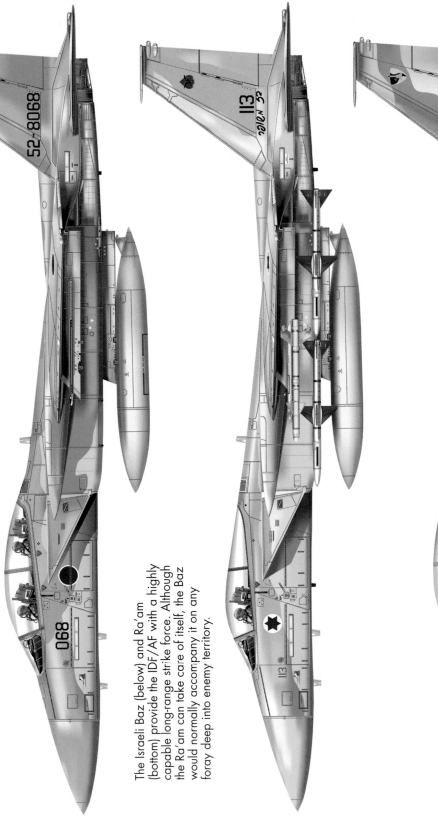

The Israeli Baz (below) and Ra'am (bottom) provide the IDF/AF with a highly capable long-range strike force. Although the Ra'am can take care of itself, the Baz would normally accompany it on any foray deep into enemy territory.

Leaving the DEEC theme, NASA 835 then moved on to Highly Integrated Digital Electronic Control (HIDEC) tests, employing a system designed to use computers to detect the loss of, or degraded use of, control surfaces. It would then reconfigure the remaining control surfaces to compensate. Simultaneously, it would alert the pilot of the failure and generate a new, real time flight envelope to help the pilot keep the aircraft flying. 835 later tested and demonstrated the Self-Repairing Flight Control System (SRFCS) in 1989 – a similar programme to NASA's HIDEC, but one which also offered analysis of failures other than those of the flight control surfaces. Electrics, hydraulics and mechanical systems were all monitored by the SRFCS, which would then make the changes necessary to reconfigure failed systems and keep the jet flying. In 1990 NASA's workhorse became involved in the Performance Seeking Control (PSC) programme; designed to optimise engine performance and ensure safe operation

Above: NASA 835 during testing of HIDEC. HIDEC was similar in concept to the PCA programme which was to follow. NASA had been interested in investigating the possibility of keeping a crippled or malfunctioning airframe airborne, despite the loss of what might have been flight-critical control surfaces. Whereas PCA investigated continued flight with every control surface inoperable, HIDEC established the feasibility of re-mapping, in flight, the flight control system to compensate for the loss of one, or several, flight control surfaces. (Boeing via Paul F. Crickmore)

Left: NASA 835 on approach during PCA testing. Complex computer algorithms were used to take commands from small thumbwheels in the cockpit (operated by the pilot), and turn them into symmetric and asymmetric increases/decreases in thrust. The system worked to such a degree that the aircraft could be landed by this method alone. (Boeing via Paul F. Crickmore)

of the engines through digital monitoring of failures and digital control of inlets, nozzles and flight controls.

NASA 835 ended its career with NASA flying the PCA (Propulsion Controlled Aircraft) programme. A series of air crashes caused by loss of flight controls had prompted NASA to begin a programme to determine whether a system could be developed to maintain control of an aircraft by simply altering thrust settings on a single engine. Initial results showed that it was certainly possible to maintain control in pitch with one engine, though asymmetric application of thrust from two engines was necessary to change heading and induce roll. Dryden and McAir took initial results, ran simulations and added a simple device to the cockpit: a two-thumbwheel control panel – one thumbwheel for required aircraft flight path, the other for bank angle. Subsequently the pilot used the thumbwheels to 'fly' the aircraft, which in turn controlled engine thrust via computer algorithms put together by NASA and McAir. The aircraft was flown down to less than 3 m (10 ft) above the runway at 150–190 kt (278–352 km/h; 164–219 mph) using these thumbwheels, and successful, hands-off, landings were made at Edwards AFB.

Appendix 1. Technical Specifications

McDonnell Douglas F-15A/B Eagle

Crew: one (two in F-15B)

Dimensions: length 19.43 m (63 ft 9 in); height 5.63 m (18 ft 5½ in); wing span 13.05 m (42 ft 9¾ in); wing area 56.48 m² (608 sq ft)

Engines: two Pratt & Whitney F100-PW-100 turbofans each rated at 65.26 kN (14,760 lb st) dry and 106 kN (23,830 lb st) with afterburning

Weights: empty equipped 12973 kg (28,600 lb); normal take-off 18884 kg (41,500 lb) on an interception mission with four AIM-7 Sparrows or 24675 kg (54,400 lb) with three 600-US gal (2271-litre) drop tanks; maximum take-off 25401 kg (56,000 lb)

Armament: M61A1 Vulcan rotary cannon in the starboard wing leading edge lip, outboard of the air intake. The gun is fed from a 940-round drum located in the central fuselage. Four AIM-9M Sidewinders (or four AIM-120 AMRAAM on MSIP aircraft) carried on the sides of the wing pylons, two to each pylon. (This arrangement allows a drop tank or bombs to be carried at the same time on the wing pylons). Four AIM-7M Sparrow SARH missiles carried on attachment points on the lower outer edges of the air intake boxes, two each side – or four AIM-120 on MSIP aircraft. Although not normally used as a bomber, the F-15 can carry up to 7257 kg (16,000 lb) of bombs, fuel tanks and missiles can be carried. The F-15 can carry 18 500-lb (227-kg) bombs, six on each wing pylon and six on the fuselage centreline

Opposite: An F-15 approaches the tanker to fill up its tanks. The F-15C's internal fuel tanks are marginally larger than those of the F-15A. (USAF)

Performance: maximum level speed 1,433 kt (2655 km/h; 1,650 mph) 'clean' at 10975 m (36,000 ft); economical cruising speed 495 kt (570 mph; 917 km/h) at optimum altitude; maximum rate of climb at sea level 15240+ m (50,000+ ft) per minute; service ceiling 18290 m (60,000 ft); absolute ceiling 30480 m (100,000 ft); ferry range with drop tanks 2,500 nm (4631 km; 2,878 miles)

McDonnell Douglas F-15C Eagle

As for F-15A except for the following:

Engines: two Pratt & Whitney F100-PW-220 turbofans each rated at 65.26 kN (14,670 lb st) dry and 106 kN (23,830 lb st) with afterburning

Weights: empty equipped 12973 kg (28,600 lb); normal take-off 20244 kg (44,630 lb) on an interception mission with four AIM-7 Sparrows or 26521 kg (58,700 lb) with three 610-US gal (2309-litre) drop tanks; maximum take-off 30844 kg (68,000 lb)

Performance: ferry range with drop tanks 2,500 nm (4633 km; 2,879 miles) without CFTs, or 3,100 nm (5745 km; 3,570 miles) with CFTs; combat radius on an interception mission 1,061 nm (1967 km; 1,222 miles)

Boeing F-15E Eagle

As for F-15C except for the following:

Crew: two

Engines: two Pratt & Whitney F100-PW-229 turbofans each rated at 79.18 kN (17,800 lb st) dry and 129.45 kN (29,100 lb st) with afterburning

Weights: empty equipped 14379 kg (31,700 lb);

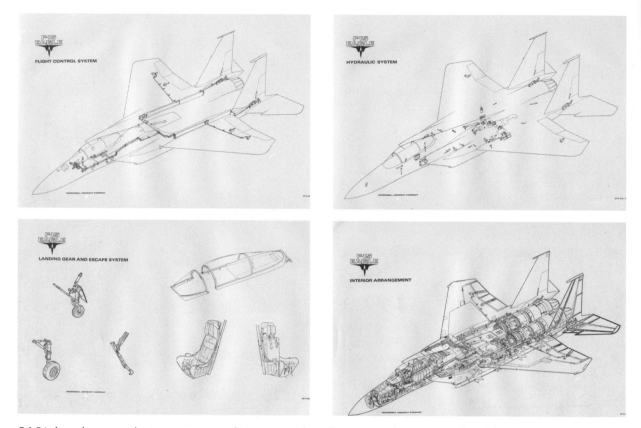

F-15A line drawings depicting systems placement and configuration. The F-15C differed from the A model in that three of its internal fuel tanks were enlarged and various additional avionics systems were added. The F-15E differs by 60 per cent from its 'light gray' cousins – new manufacturing techniques were developed to give its airframe a 16,000-hour life cycle and a sustained 9g turn capability. (Boeing via Steve Davies)

maximum take-off 36741 kg (81,000 lb)

Armament: M61A1 Vulcan rotary cannon in the starboard wing leading edge lip, outboard of the air intake. The gun is fed from a 512-round drum located in the central fuselage. Four AIM-9M Sidewinders carried on the sides of the wing pylons. Up to 11000 kg (24,250 lb) of bombs, fuel

The F-15 is a big fighter – standing on the top of an F-15's wing for the first time is a jaw dropping experience – there is some truth in the legend that the surface area is the size of a tennis court! An F-16 and F-15C from Spangdhalem AB, Germany, fly in close formation to demonstrate this. Despite its size, F-16 pilots must remain focused during air combat manoeuvring against the F-15 – USAF Eagle squadrons are among the best fighter squadrons in the world, their pilots are highly trained and capable of crushing more nimble fighters which employ the wrong tactics. (USAF)

Right: The F-15E is visually distinguishable from its brethren for a number of reasons: its tail hook has no cover, small bulges are visible on the main undercarriage doors, it features a significantly different cockpit, both tail booms carry ALQ-135 antennas, it carries tangential CFTs with associates munitions loading stations as standard, and it uses a wide field of view HUD. (USAF)

The F-15E Strike Eagle features an uprated undercarriage to cope with the additional weight of the airframe and air-to-ground weapons. In addition, the tyres are enlarged, giving rise to a small bulge being added to the main gear doors to accommodate them. The nose landing gear (NLG) of the F-15E, which differs only slightly from that on all other F-15 models, is shown below. An F-15A main landing gear (MLG) strut is shown below right. (Steve Davies (below) and Dennis R. Jenkins)

tanks and missiles can be carried on two wing pylons, underfuselage pylons and 12 bomb racks mounted directly on the CFTs. AIM-7 and AIM-120 air-to-air missiles can also be carried, as on the F-15C.

Undercarriage specifications:

Wheel track	2.75 m (9 ft ¼ in)
Wheel base	5.42 m (17 ft 9½ in)
Tyre size (nose)	22 x 7.75–9
Tyre size (main)	36 x 11–18
Tyre pressure	21 bar (305 psi)

F100-PW-229 specifications:

Thrust (dry)	79.18 kN (17,800 lb st)
Thrust (A-B)	129.45 kN (29,100 lb st)
Weight	1696 kg (3,740 lb)
Length	4.82 m (15 ft 9½ in)
Inlet Diameter	0.86 m (2 ft 10 in)
Maximum diameter	1.17 m (3 ft 10 in)
Bypass ratio	0.36:1
Overall pressure ratio	32:1

Control surface areas:

Ailerons	2.46 m² (26.48 sq ft)
Flaps	3.33 m² (35.84 sq ft)
Horizontal Stabilisers	10.35 m² (111.36 sq ft)
Vertical Stabilisers	9.78 m² (105.28 sq ft)
Rudders	1.85 m² (19.94 sq ft)

Wing specifications:

Wing area	56.48 m² (608 sq ft)
Wing sweep	45°
Aspect ratio	3
Anhedral	1°
Max loading	650 kg/m² (133.20 lb/sq ft)

AN/AAQ-13 Navigation Pod specifications:

Length	1.99 m (78⅛ in)
Diameter	0.31 m (12 in)
Weight	211.50 kg (470 lb)
Unit cost	$1.38 million

AN/AAQ-14 Targeting Pod specifications:

Length	2.51 m (98½ in)
Diameter	0.38 m (15 in)
Weight	235.80 kg (524 lb)
Unit Cost	$3.2 million

F-15 variants

F-15A: Initial single-seat version for USAF and Israel with F100-PW-100 engines and APG-63 radar. Note: Initial development aircraft designated F-15A not YF-15

F-15A/B MSIP: Minor update to USAF fleet during the 1980s
TF-15A: Initial designation for F-15B
F-15B: First two-seat trainer version. Fully mission capable but without the F-15A's AN/ALQ-135 ECM equipment
F-15A/B MSIP II: Upgrade to near F-15C/D standard for USAF aircraft during the 1990s, with APG-70 radar, new avionics and digital

The F100 engine has eventually proved to be a success for the USAF. Representing a quantum leap forward in technology, the F100-PW-100 was the first mark used in production F-15s. The latest version is the PW-229, the engine fitted to a select number of F-15Es. This photograph shows the afterburner, variable exhaust nozzle section of the PW-229. These complex nozzles used to be covered by twelve titanium strips known as 'Turkey feathers', as a means of protecting the system and reducing drag. The 'feathers' proved to be a maintenance headache however, and were removed from USAF F-15s. Some Israeli aircraft retain them. (Both Steve Davies)

The F-15E Strike Eagle's cockpit differs massively from that of other F-15 variants. Gone are the older-style mechanical gauges. Instead, each cockpit is fitted with Sperry multi-function displays. These displays are officially called MPDs, and the front cockpit has three (one colour), and the rear cockpit four (two colour). Noteworthy in these photographs are the push buttons around the displays, which allow aircrew to select on-screen display options such as going to the main menu or switching a display from the radar screen to the TP image. The displays can be programmed to scroll through certain pages (in a user-defined sequence) at the touch of a button on either of the WSO's hand controllers (mounted either side of the seat and used to control aircraft systems and sensors) or the pilot's control stick. (Steve Davies)

computers replacing the original analogue computers

F-15C: Improved single-seater for USAF with increased internal fuel, updated APG-63 radar and provision for CFTs along the sides of the intakes. Initial aircraft had F100-PW-100 engines, but most were delivered with F100-PW-220 standard engines

F-15D: Two-seat version of F-15C

F-15C/D MSIP: Avionics upgrade for USAF aircraft with new APG-70 radar, cockpit displays, EW systems and digital computers

F-15DJ: Two-seat version of F-15D for Japan

TF-15A 'Strike Eagle': Second development TF-15A modified during 1982 for dedicated air-to-ground operations to potentially replace the F-111. Company-funded demonstrator

F-15E: Production two-seater with dedicated all-weather ground attack capability. Features strengthened airframe, redesigned cockpit, improved avionics and (in later production and retrofit) uprated F100-PW-229 engines. Note: 'Strike Eagle' name not officially adopted by the USAF

F-15I Ra'am (thunder): Export version of F-15E for Israel with significant Israeli avionics fit

The rear cockpit shown here has been configured for Night Vision Goggle lighting – this consists of filters installed over the two outer MPCDs, a filter over the Up Front Controller panel, and filters over the 'brow' warning lights. In addition to this, small green tubes are attached below the centre MPDs by means of Velcro. The tubes contain chemical sticks which shine light over the back-up instruments below. (Steve Davies)

F-15J: Single-seater for Japan based on F-15C with some local avionics

F-15S: Export version of F-15E for Saudi Arabia with downgraded avionics

F-15F: Proposed single-seat fighter version of F-15E for Saudi Arabia

F-15H: Proposed export version of F-15E for Saudi Arabia with reduced sensor fit

F-15K: Advanced F-15E model for South Korea

F-15XP: Initial generic designation for F-15F/H export versions of F-15E for Saudi Arabia

NF-15B 'Agile Eagle': F-15B used for manoeuvre-control research

F-15N 'Sea Eagle': Proposed version for US Navy

F-15XX: Proposed lightweight development of F-15C with improved avionics and systems, as a low-cost alternative to the F-22 for the USAF. Abandoned in 1992

RF-15 'Peak Eagle': Proposed dedicated reconnaissance version

F-15C Wild Weasel: Proposed defence suppression version

F-15/PDF: Planned conversion of F-15Cs to defence suppression role as Precision Direction Finder (PDF) aircraft. Proposed for aircraft replaced by the F-22

SMTD Eagle: First F-15B development aircraft modified by NASA for flight control research. Fitted with canards and 2D thrust vectoring exhaust nozzles

Appendix 2. Weapons and Stores

Both the F-15A/B/C/D and F-15E variants are cleared to carry an almost identical list of air-to-air and air-to-ground ordnance. The F-15A/B/C/D officially discontinued its air to ground role in 1992 as a result of the widespread introduction of the F-15E into USAF service. The list below details the weapons cleared for carriage by both types in USAF service, with those cleared on the F-15E only highlighted <u>thus</u>. Stores loading and station information below is for the F-15A through to D without CFTs installed. The loading configuration for the F-15E is significantly different.

Finally, it should be noted that while A through to D model Eagles may have been certified to carry certain stores (such as AGM-65), the USAF only trained and used a limited variety of these. Where the F-15A/B/C/D is certified to carry a particular store but the author has been unable to find information on the configuration in which it would be carried, a * symbol has been inserted.

URITS/ACMI Training Pods

The Rangeless Interim Training System (URITS) is designated AN/ASQ-T38. It is used by the USAFE as a cheaper alternative to ACMI, and provides the following capabilities: pod-to-pod communications, state-of-the-art display and debriefing stations, unparalleled time-space position accuracy, real-time monitoring (optional), interoperability with NATO forces, no drop weapon scoring (NDWS) (optional), real-time kill notification (RTKN), safety advisories (optional) and high fidelity weapons simulation.

Utilising GPS, URITS processes and stores data on aircraft position, velocity, altitude, and simulated weapons firing and release. The ground-based debriefing station consists of computer equipment capable of real-time transmission of the fight sequence. Since the majority of the computer systems that make up URITS are placed within the airborne pods, the system reduces the need to confine training to a given combat range or airspace. As a result, URITS is described as an 'untethered' or 'rangeless' system.

The URITS contract was awarded to Metric on 19 February 1999, following an open competition between Metric and Cubic – two US-owned electronics manufacturers. Metric has been supplying pods to USAFE under the URITS

A URITS pod seen mounted on an F-15E. The pod is a self-contained unit which can be used without the need for complex and expensive instrumented ranges. Note the inert AIM-9L and 610-US gal (2271-litre) fuel tank. (Steve Davies)

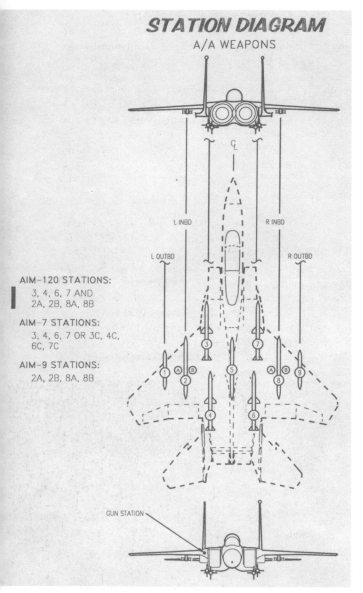

STATION DIAGRAM
A/A WEAPONS

L INBD R INBD

L OUTBD R OUTBD

AIM–120 STATIONS:
3, 4, 6, 7 AND
2A, 2B, 8A, 8B

AIM-7 STATIONS:
3, 4, 6, 7 OR 3C, 4C,
6C, 7C

AIM-9 STATIONS:
2A, 2B, 8A, 8B

GUN STATION

instrumented ranges. It lacks the ability of URITS to work 'anywhere', as it requires ground stations to receive and record data transmitted from the pod. It does offer some advantages over URITS however, namely that it offers better range and increased sophistication in playback/debriefing options. The most recent ACMI pod is the Metric AN/ASQ-T27 P4B Airborne Instrumentation System (AIS) pod.

AIM-7 Sparrow (F/M and F-3)

The Sparrow is an SARH air-to-air missile, it features BVR capability and was originally designed to intercept Soviet strategic bombers. The AIM-7M features improved 'look-down/shoot-down' capabilities, as well as resistance to ECM. Up to four Sparrow missiles may be carried by the F-15 on stations 3, 4, 6 and 7.

Weights: 231 kg (510 lb); warhead 39 kg (86 lb)
Dimensions: length 3.60 m (11 ft 10 in); diameter 203 mm (8 in); wing span 1.02 m (3 ft 4 in); tail span 0.81 m (2 ft 8 in)
Performance: speed Mach 4+; maximum range approximately 30 nm (56 km; 34.5 miles)
Propulsion: Hercules Mk 58 or Aerojet General Mk 65 boost-sustained solid-fuel rocket
Configuration: long cylinder with pointed nose, two sets of cruciform delta wings indexed in line, the steerable foreplanes at mid-body and another fixed set at the tail
Warhead: Mk 71 controlled fragmentation high-explosive
Sensors/Fire control: inverse monopulse semi-active radar homing seeker with digital signal processor, improved autopilot and fuse (which can work as contact or proximity type). Upgrades provide better ECM resistance, improved 'look-down/shoot-down' capability.

AIM-120 AMRAAM (A, B and C)

The AIM-120 AMRAAM is a new-generation AAM. It has an all-weather, BVR capability. AMRAAM employs active radar target tracking, proportional navigation guidance, and active radio frequency target detection. It employs

contract on a compressed delivery schedule since 20 May 1999. Under the terms of the contract, a total of 88 pods and eleven debriefing stations are to be phased-in at three locations in Europe, and at a fourth site later determined to be Saudi Arabia.

ACMI

ACMI is an Air Combat Manoeuvring Instrumentation system that relies on active, semi-active, and inertial navigational methods of guidance to provide an autonomous launch-and-leave capability against single and multiple targets in all environments.

The AIM-120A is a non-reprogrammable missile (it requires a hardware change to upgrade the missile software). The AIM-120B/C is reprogrammable through the missile umbilical using Common Field-level Memory Reprogramming Equipment (CFMRE). The AIM-120C has smaller control surfaces to enable internal carriage on the F-22. Up to eight AIM-120s may be carried by the F-15 on stations 3, 4, 6, 7, 2A, 2B, 8A and 8B.

Weights: launch 150.75 kg (335 lb)
Dimensions: length 366 cm (143⁹⁄₁₀ in); diameter 17.78 cm (7 in); wing span 52.58 cm (20⁷⁄₁₀ in)
Performance: range: 32+ km (20+ miles); speed supersonic
Powerplant: high performance
Warhead: blast fragmentation
Guidance system: Active radar, terminal/ inertial midcourse
Unit cost: $386,000

Right: A trolley of inert AIM-120 AMRAAM and AIM-9L Sidewinder missiles awaiting loading onto an F-15E. The AIM-7 Sparrow had suffered greatly from general wear and tear during the war in SEA. It had not been manufactured to survive the rigours of tens of take-offs and landings, and, as a consequence, component failure was a major factor in the dismal success rate accredited to it. The AIM-120 has been designed from the outset with a good tolerance to hundreds or even thousands of 'captive carry' sorties. (Steve Davies)

AIM-9 Sidewinder (P, L and M)

The AIM-9 Sidewinder is a supersonic, heat-seeking, air-to-air missile. It has a high-explosive warhead and an active infra-red guidance system. The AIM-9M, currently the only operational variant, has the all-aspect capability of the L model, but provides all-around higher performance. The M model has improved defence against infra-red countermeasures, enhanced background discrimination capability, and a reduced-smoke rocket motor. Up to four may be carried by the F-15 on stations 2A, 2B, 8A and 8B.

Weights: launch 85.5 kg (190 lb); warhead 11.34-kg (25-lb) high explosive for AIM-9H' 9.43-kg (20.8-lb) high explosive for AIM-9L/M
Dimensions: length 2.87 m (9 ft 5 in); diameter 0.13 m (5 in); fin span 0.63 m (2 ft ¾ in)
Performance: speed Mach 2.5; range 16 to 29 km (10 to 18 miles) depending on altitude
Powerplant: Hercules and Bermite Mk 36 Mod 71, 8 solid-propellant rocket motor
Warhead: annular blast fragmentation

Left: The seeker head of an inert AIM-9L. The AIM-9 has progressed from being a primitive IR AAM to being a deadly, highly agile all aspect missile. The AIM-9X, which should be integrated into the F-15C and F-15E, provides high off-boresight (high angle) tracking and intercept capabilities. The missile's 'umbilical' can be clearly seen in this picture – it is attached to a plug in the missile launch rail and is used to send data to and from the aircraft prior to launch. (Steve Davies)

Guidance system: solid-state, infra-red homing system
Unit cost: approximately $84,000

M61A1 Vulcan 20-mm cannon

The M61A1 Vulcan cannon is a six-barrel 20-mm weapon capable of firing 6,600 rounds per minute. Its operation is based upon the principle used in the rapid-firing gun invented by Richard J Gatling in the 1860s. The six rotating barrels, firing one at a time, permit a high rate of fire while at the same time reducing the problem of barrel wear and heat generation. The gun can be driven electrically, hydraulically, or by a ram-air turbine. Some 512 rounds may be carried by the F-15E (although later aircraft only have space for about 450 rounds), and 940 rounds may be carried by all other F-15 variants.

Fuel tanks

610-US gallon (2271-litre) fuel tanks may be carried for ferry flight or where long-range missions dictate additional fuel must be carried. A maximum of three tanks (or 'bags' as they are known to aircrew) may be carried, one each on stations 2, 5 and 8. F-15Cs are often seen with a single centreline fuel tank to allow extended training sorties to be flown.

MXU-648 Travel Pod

Used to carry personal belongings, small pieces of maintenance equipment or beer! A maximum of three may be carried, one each on stations 2, 5 and 8.

ECM pods

All US versions of the F-15 carry the AN/ALQ-135 ICS as part of the TEWS system. As such, external jamming pods are unnecessary. Provision has been made for the following systems, however: AN/ALQ-119(V)-12; AN/ALQ-184(V)-1/2/3/4/5/6/7/8; AN/ALQ-131(V)-4/5/6/9/10/12/ 13/14/15 and AN/ALQ-176. All may be carried singularly on station 5, while AN/ALQ-188 and AN/ALQ-188A(V) may be carried on either stations 2 or 8.

SUU-20B/A Training Pod

In peacetime, small, blue BDU-33 bomblets which closely simulate the ballistics of Mk 82 LDGP bombs are used for training. Each bomblet carries a small smoke charge which detonates on impact with the ground, releasing a cloud of smoke to allow range controllers to accurately 'score' the accuracy of the drop. Up to 18 BDU-33B bomblets may be carried on Multiple Ejection Racks (MERs) on stations 2, 5 and 8. Alternatively, three SUU-20B/A pods may be carried on the same stations. Each SUU-20 carries 6 BDU-33 rounds.

AN/AXQ-14 DLP (Data Link Pod) *

This pod acts as the interface between the GBU-15 or AGM-130 PGM and the aircraft. Used principally by the F-15E, the DLP transmits steering data to the bomb from the jet and imagery from the bomb's seeker to the jet. In addition, the AN/AXQ-14 may be used to transmit and receive near real-time imagery to and from control centres via secure satellite uplinks. The pod is referred to by the F-15E community as 'Gold Pan'. The F-15A/B/C/D are also cleared to carry the pod.

Mk 82 LDGP, Mk 82 AIR (BSU-49 fin) & Mk 82 Snakeye (Mk 18 fin)

The Mk 82 is a free-fall, unguided general purpose [GP] 500-lb (227-kg) bomb. The bomb is usually equipped with the mechanical M904 (nose) and M905 (tail) fuses or the radar-proximity FMU-113 air-burst fuse. The Mk 80-series LDGP bombs are used in the majority of bombing operations where maximum blast and explosive effects are desired. Their cases are relatively light and approximately 45 per cent of their complete weight is explosive. General purpose bombs may use both nose and tail fuses and conical or retarded tail fins.

The Mk 82 AIR is modified with a BSU-49/B high drag tail assembly. The 'ballute' air bag which deploys from the tail provides a high-speed, low-altitude delivery capability, by quickly slowing the bomb and allowing the aircraft to escape its blast pattern. The tail assembly consists of a low-drag canister unit containing a ballute (combination balloon and parachute), and a release lanyard assembly that opens the canister to release the ballute. The ballute assembly is made from high-strength, low-porosity nylon fabric. When the bomb is

Right: Weapons specialists load the seeker head unit onto a Mk 84 2,000-lb LDGP bomb. When fused, and with the tail unit mated to the bomb casing, the entire assembly is subsequently designated GBU-10. This prolific weapon is starting to show its age, yet remains the staple weapon of choice for attacking low-value targets with precision. (Steve Davies)

released from the aircraft, a lanyard unlatches the back cover of the tail, which opens, releasing part of the nylon bag/retarder. Air turbulence at the rear of the bomb acts on that portion of the retarder, pulling the remainder out of the housing. Ram air inflation is accomplished through four air inlet ports toward the aft end of the ballute. The weapon can be delivered in the low-drag mode (canister remains closed after release) or in the high drag mode; this is cockpit selectable depending on mission requirements.

Up to eighteen Mk 82 series bombs can be carried on BRU-26A MERs. Stations 2, 5 and 8 are used.

Mk 83 LDGP

The Mk 83 is very similar to the Mk 82 series, but carries a 1,000-lb (454-kg) explosive charge. It is carried singularly on stations 2, 5 and 8.

Mk 84 LDGP and Mk 84 AIR (BSU-50/B fin)

Again, very similar to the Mk 82- and Mk 83-series bombs, but with a 2,000-lb (907-kg) charge. Many of the more than 12,000 Mk 84s expended during *Desert Storm* were dropped by USAF F-15Es. A maximum of three is carried, one each on stations 2, 5 and 8.

AGM-65 Maverick (A, B, D & G) *

The AGM-65 Maverick is a tactical, air-to-surface guided missile designed for close air support, interdiction and defence suppression missions. It provides stand-off capability and high probability of strike against a wide range of tactical targets, including armour, air defences, ships, transportation equipment and fuel storage facilities. The AGM-65 is modular in design and there are several different versions in use today: AGM-65D has an imaging infra-red guidance system that features adverse weather capabilities. It can track heat generated by a target and provide the pilot with a pictorial display of the target during darkness, or in hazy

or inclement weather; AGM-65G has essentially the same guidance system as the D, but with software modifications that allow it to track larger targets. The G model's major difference is its heavyweight penetrator warhead, while Maverick B and D models employ the shaped-charge warhead.

The F-15E used the AGM-65 with great success, towards the end of Operation *Desert Storm*.

GBU-10 LGB

The Guided Bomb Unit-10 (GBU-10) utilises the 2,000-lb Mk 84 or BLU-109 penetrating warhead. The munition guides to a spot of laser energy reflected from a target.

The GBU-10I mates a BLU-109B warhead with a Paveway II laser guidance kit. This improved 2,000-lb bomb is used against targets requiring deeper penetration. The GBU-10 is cleared for singular carriage on stations 2, 5 and 8.

GBU-12 LGB *

A 500-lb LGB used extensively in operations since *Desert Storm*. There are two generations of GBU-12 LGBs – Paveway I with fixed wings and Paveway II with folding wings. Paveway II models have their detector optics and housing made of injection-moulded plastic to reduce weight and cost; increased detector sensitivity; reduced thermal battery delay after release; increased maximum canard deflection; laser coding; folding wings for carriage; and increased detector field of view. (Paveway II's instantaneous field of view is 30 per cent greater than that of Paveway I.)

LANTIRN provides an infra-red image to the crew for the purposes of finding targets, and then targeting and guiding LGBs onto them. This image was taken from the WSO's cockpit and shows the TP image the crew gets. Three zoom settings are available, and the crew can also change the polarity of the image from 'black=hot' to 'white=hot'. (Steve Davies)

GBU-15 EO-guided bomb *

The GBU-15 can deliver either a Mk 84 GP or a BLU-109B penetrating warhead with pinpoint accuracy via data link control from low to high altitude at a significant stand-off distance. It is equipped with either a television or an imaging infra-red seeker. The seeker provides the launch aircraft with visual presentation of the target and surroundings as seen from the weapon. During free flight, this presentation is transmitted by a two-way data link system via the AN/AXQ-14 pod to the aircraft's cockpit television monitor. The seeker can be locked onto the target either before or after launch, for automatic weapon guidance, or it can be manually steered by the WSO.

GBU-24 LGB *

The GBU-24 Low-Level Laser-Guided Bomb [LLLGB] consists of either a Mk 84 or BLU-109 warhead with a Paveway III kit. Paveway III employs proportional guidance in place of the 'bang-bang' guidance used by Paveway I and II. The LLLGB was developed in response to sophisticated enemy air defences and poor visibility, and to counter limitations under low ceilings. It is designed for low-altitude delivery and with a capability for improved stand-off ranges to reduce exposure. Performance envelopes for all modes of delivery are improved because the larger wings of the GBU-24 increase manoeuvrability. Paveway III also has increased seeker sensitivity and a larger field of regard.

GBU-28 LGB

The GBU-28 is a special weapon, originally developed for penetrating hardened Iraqi command centres located deep underground. It is a 5,000-lb (2268-kg) LGB with a 4,400-lb (1996-kg) penetrating warhead. The bombs are modified Army artillery tubes and contain 630 lb (286 kg) of high explosives. They are fitted with GBU-27 LGB kits, 0.37 m (14½ in) in diameter and almost 5.79 m (19 ft) long.

AGM-130 TV/IR missile

The adverse weather AGM-130 provides advanced combat capabilities, including 24-hour strike capability with a new INS/GPS guidance system coupled with a state-of-the-art Imaging Infra-Red Focal Plane Array Seeker.

The CBU range

CBU-52 *: SUU-30 dispenser containing 220 anti-matériel, anti-personnel bomblets. It weighs 356 kg (785 lb) and can be used with a variety of proximity fuses or the mechanical Mk 339 timed fuse. The submunition is a 8.89-cm (3.5-in) diameter spherical bomblet weighing 1.22 kg (2.7 lb) with a 0.29-kg (0.65-lb) high-explosive warhead

CBU-58 *: SUU-30 dispenser; 650 bomblets. These bomblets contain 5-g (0.2-oz) titanium pellets, making them incendiary and useful against flammable targets

CBU-71 *: SUU-30 dispenser; 650 BLU-68/B incendiary submunitions which use titanium pellets as the incendiary agent. The bomblet has two separate kill mechanisms, one fragmentation, the other incendiary. Both incorporate a time delay fuse, which detonates at random times after impact

CBU-87: The CBU-87 is a 1,000-lb (454-kg) Combined Effects Munition (CEM) for attacking soft target areas with detonating bomblets. It is an all-purpose cluster weapons system, and consists of an SW-65 Tactical Munitions Dispenser (TMD) with an optional FZU-39 proximity sensor. The BLU-97/B Combined Effects Bomb (CEB), effective against armour, personnel and matériel, contains a shaped charge, scored steel casing and zirconium ring for anti-armour, fragmentation and incendiary capability. The bomblet case is made of scored steel designed to break into approximately 300 preformed ingrain fragments for defeating light armour and personnel. A total of 202 of these bomblets are loaded in each dispenser, enabling a single payload attack against a variety of targets and wide-area coverage. The footprint of the CBU-87 is approximately 200 m x 400 m (656 ft x 1312 ft). The body of the submunition is cylindrical in shape, approximately 20 cm (7.87 in) long, and 6 cm (2.36 in) in diameter.

CBU-89: The CBU-89 Gator mine, a 1,000-lb cluster munition containing anti-tank and anti-personnel mines, consists of an SUU-64 Tactical Munitions Dispenser with 72 anti-tank mines, 22 anti-personnel mines, and an optional FZU-39 proximity sensor. Mine arming begins when the dispenser opens. Mine detonation is initiated by target detection, mine disturbance, low battery voltage, or a self-destruct time-out. The anti-tank mine is a magnetic sensing submunition effective against tanks and armoured vehicles. The anti-personnel mine has a fragmenting case warhead triggered by trip wires.

CBU-92: A 431-kg (950-lb) ERAM (Extended-Range Anti-Armour Munition) anti-tank cluster bomb (nine BLU-108/B submunitions and three area-denial submunitions in an SUU-65/B canister)

The AGM-130 is a huge weapon with an impressive stand-off range. This inert unit sits ready for training purposes. Below the Mk 84 bomb casing is the rocket motor. This motor has a burn time of one minute and can be set to fire from the moment of launch, or to delay firing until the weapon slows below a certain speed. Upon completion of the motor burn time, a small charge ejects the spent canister from the main bomb. (Steve Davies)

Mk 20 Rockeye CBU: The Mk 20 Rockeye is a free-fall, unguided cluster weapon designed to kill tanks and armoured vehicles. The system consists of a clamshell dispenser, a mechanical Mk 339 timed fuse, and 247 dual-purpose armour-piercing, shaped-charge bomblets. The bomblet weighs 0.60 kg (1.32 lb) and has a 0.18-kg (0.4-lb) shaped-charge, high-explosive warhead, which produces up to 17250 bar (250,000 psi) at the point of impact, allowing the penetration of approximately 19 cm (7½ in) of armour. Rockeye is most efficiently used against area targets requiring penetration to kill. Up to eighteen Rockeyes can be carried on stations 2, 5 and 8.

B61 nuclear bomb *

The B61 can be dropped at high speeds from altitudes as low as 15 m (50 ft). It can be dropped either free-fall or parachute-retarded; it can be detonated either by air burst or ground burst. The retarded ground burst delivery is also called 'laydown' because the weapon lies on the ground for a period before detonation. This allows the delivery aircraft to escape.

Weight: 322 kg (710 lb)
Dimensions: length 3.59 m (11 ft 9½ in); diameter 33.87 cm (13.4 in)
Yield: kiloton range

Appendix 3. Production Figures

McDonnell Douglas Aircraft Corporation (McAir). Later Boeing Military Aircraft

Version	Quantity	Location	Time
F-15A	384	St Louis	1972–1979
F-15B	61	St Louis	1972–1979
F-15C	483	St Louis	1979–1985
F-15D	92	St Louis	1979–1985
F-15J	2	St Louis	1979–1980
F-15DJ	12	St Louis	1979–1981
F-15E	237	St Louis	1985–c.2003
F-15I	25	St Louis	1996–1998
F-15S	72	St Louis	1996–1998
F-15K	40	St Louis	c.2005–2008

Total: 1,408

Mitsubishi Heavy Industries Ltd

Version	Quantity	Location	Time
F-15J	139	Tokyo	1981–1997
F-15DJ	25	Tokyo	1981–1997

Total: 164

Total Produced: 1,572 aircraft

Serial	Version	Notes
71-0280/0281	F-15A-1-MC	'281 bailed to NASA in 1975, Returned to USAF in 1983
71-0282/0284	F-15A-2-MC	'284 to GF-15A
71-0285/0286	F-15A-3-MC	'286 to GF-15A
71-0287/0289	F-15A-4-MC	'287 bailed to NASA in 1976 as 835

Serial	Version	Notes	Serial	Version	Notes
72-0113/0116	F-15A-5-MC	'116 delivered to Israel, *Peace Fox I*	71-0291	F-15B-4-MC	used for FAST Pack, CFT and LANTIRN evaluation. Became F-15E development aircraft
72-0117/0120	F-15A-6-MC	'117,'118 delivered to Israel, *Peace Fox I*; '119 Operation *Streak Eagle*; '120 delivered to Israel, *Peace Fox I*	73-0108/0110	F-15B-7-MC	
			73-0111/0112	F-15B-8-MC	
			73-0113/0114	F-15B-9-MC	
			74-0137/0138	F-15B-10-MC	
			74-0139/0140	F-15B-11-MC	
73-0085/0089	F-15A-7-MC		74-0141/0142	F-15B-12-MC	
73-0090/0097	F-15A-8-MC		74-0143/0157	F-15A/B	cancelled contract
73-0098/0107	F-15A-9-MC				
74-0081/0093	F-15A-10-MC		75-0080/0084	F-15B-13-MC	
74-0094/0111	F-15A-11-MC		75-0085/0089	F-15B-14-MC	
74-0112/0136	F-15A-12-MC		75-0090/0124	F-15A/B	cancelled contract
74-0143/0157	F-15A/B	cancelled contract			
75-0018/0048	F-15A-13-MC		76-0124/0129	F-15B-15-MC	
75-0049/0079	F-15A-14-MC		76-0130/0135	F-15B-16-MC	
75-0090/0124	F-15A/B	cancelled contract	76-0136/0140	F-15B-17-MC	
			76-0141/0142	F-15B-18-MC	
76-0008/0046	F-15A-15-MC		76-1524/1525	F-15B-16-MC	for Israel, *Peace Fox II*
76-0047/0083	F-15A-16-MC				
76-0084/0113	F-15A-17-MC	'086 used for trials with ASM-135A ASAT	77-0154/0156	F-15B-18-MC	
			77-0157/0162	F-15B-19-MC	
			77-0163/0168	F-15B-20-MC	'166 used as test vehicle for Integrated Flight Control/Firefly III programme
76-0114/0120	F-15A-18-MC	'120 delivered to Israel			
76-0121/0123	F-15A	cancelled contract			
76-1505/1514	F-15A-17-MC	for Israel, *Peace Fox II*	78-0468/0495	F-15C-21-MC	
			78-0496/0522	F-15C-22-MC	
76-1515/1523	F-15A-18-MC	for Israel, *Peace Fox II*	78-0523/0550	F-15C-23-MC	
			78-0551/0560	F-15C Eagle	cancelled contract
77-0061/0084	F-15A-18-MC	'084 used as test bed for APG-63 radar	79-0015/0037	F-15C-24-MC	0015, 0017/ 0019, 0023/ 0024, 0028, 0031/0033 to Saudi Arabia
77-0085/0119	F-15A-19-MC				
77-0120/0153	F-15A-20-MC				
			79-0038/0058	F-15C-25-MC	0038/ 0039, 0043, 0045, 0051/0052, 0055 to Saudi Arabia
71-0290	F-15B-3-MC	Modified as part of SMTD programme (Agile Eagle)			

Serial	Version	Notes	Serial	Version	Notes
79-0059/0081	F-15C-26-MC	0060, 0062/ 0063 to Saudi Arabia	85-0093/0107	F-15C-39-MC	'102 credited with 3 kills in Gulf War
80-0002/0023	F-15C-27-MC		85-0108/0128	85-0108/0128	
80-0024/0038	F-15C-28-MC		85-0132/0134	F-15C-40-MC	
80-0039/0053	F-15C-29-MC		86-0143/0162	F-15C-41-MC	
80-0062/0067	F-15C-28-MC	for Saudi Arabia, *Peace Sun*	86-0163/0180	F-15C-42-MC	
			90-263/268	F-15C-49-MC	for Saudi Arabia, *Peace Sun*
80-0068/0074	F-15C-29-MC	for Saudi Arabia, *Peace Sun*	90-269/271	F-15C-50-MC	for Saudi Arabia, *Peace Sun*
80-0075/0085	F-15C-30-MC	for Saudi Arabia, *Peace Sun*			
80-0086/0099	F-15C-31-MC	for Saudi Arabia, *Peace Sun*	78-0561/0565	F-15D-21-MC	
			78-0566/0570	F-15D-22-MC	
			78-0571/0574	F-15D-23-MC	
80-0100/0106	F-15C-32-MC	for Saudi Arabia, *Peace Sun*	78-0575	F-15D	cancelled contract all to Saudi Arabia
80-0122/0124	F-15C-27-MC	for Israel, *Peace Fox III*	79-0004/0006	F-15D-24-MC	
			79-0007/0011	F-15D-25-MC	
80-0125/0127	F-15C-28-MC	for Israel, *Peace Fox III*	79-0012/0014	F-15D-26-MC	
			80-0054/0055	F-15D-27-MC	
80-0128/0130	F-15C-29-MC	for Israel, *Peace Fox III*	80-0056/0057	F-15D-28-MC	
			80-0058/0061	F-15D-29-MC	
81-0002	F-15C-32-MC	for RSAF	80-0107/0110	F-15D-27-MC	for Saudi Arabia, *Peace Sun*
81-0020/0031	F-15C-30-MC				
81-0032/0040	F-15C-31-MC				
81-0041/0056	F-15C-32-MC		80-0111/0112	F-15D-28-MC	for Saudi Arabia, *Peace Sun*
81-0057/0060	F-15C	cancelled contract			
82-0008/0022	F-15C-33-MC		80-0113/0114	F-15D-29-MC	for Saudi Arabia, *Peace Sun*
82-0023/0038	F-15C-34-MC				
83-0010/0034	F-15C-35-MC		80-0115/0117	F-15D-30-MC	for Saudi Arabia, *Peace Sun*
83-0035/0043	F-15C-36-MC				
83-0044/0045	F-15C	cancelled contract	80-0118/0119	F-15D-31-MC	for Saudi Arabia, *Peace Sun*
83-0054/0055	F-15C-35-MC	for Israel, *Peace Fox III*			
83-0056/0062	F-15C-36-MC	for Israel, *Peace Fox III*	80-0120/0121	F-15D-32-MC	for Saudi Arabia, *Peace Sun*
84-0001/0015	F-15C-37-MC				
84-0016/0031	F-15C-38-MC		80-0131/0132	F-15D-27-MC	for Israel, *Peace Fox III*
84-0032/0041	F-15C	cancelled contract	80-0133/0136	F-15D-28-MC	for Israel, *Peace Fox III*

Serial	Version	Notes
81-0003	F-15D-32-MC	for Saudi Arabia
81-0061/0062	F-15D-30-MC	
81-0063/0065	F-15D-31-MC	
81-0066/0067	F-15D	cancelled contract
82-0044/0045	F-15D-33-MC	
82-0046/0048	F-15D-34-MC	
83-0046/0048	F-15D-35-MC	
83-0049/0050	F-15D-36-MC	
83-0063/0064	F-15D-35-MC	for Israel, *Peace Fox III*
84-0042/0044	F-15D-37-MC	
84-0045/0046	F-15D-38-MC	
84-0047/0048	F-15D	cancelled contract
85-0139/0131	F-15D-39-MC	
86-0181/0182	F-15D-41-MC	

Serial	Version	Notes
71-0291	F-15B-4-MC	development aircraft
86-0183/0184	F-15E-41-MC	
86-0185/0190	F-15E-42-MC	
87-0169/0189	F-15E-43-MC	
87-0190/0210	F-15E-44-MC	
87-0211/0216	F-15E	cancelled contract
88-1667/1687	F-15E-45-MC	
88-1688/1708	F-15E-45-MC	
89-0471/0506	F-15E	
90-0227/0262	F-15E	
91-0300/0335	F-15E	
92-0607/0608	F-15E	
96-200/205	F-15E-58-MC	
	F-15E-61-MC	
	F-15E-62-MC	

Appendix 4. Museum Aircraft

All museums are in the USA unless noted otherwise:

Location	Version	Serial	Notes
Hill Aerospace Museum	F-15A	77-0090	
Warner Robins Museum of Aviation	F-15A	71-0280	first production F-15A
Langley AFB	F-15A	71-0281	ex-NASA
IWM Duxford, England	F-15A	76-0020	

Location	Version	Serial	Notes
RAF Lakenheath England	F-15A	74-00131	as '92-048'
Air Force Armament Museum	F-15A		
Robins AFB Museum of Aviation	F-15A	73-0099	working lights
Octave Chanute Aerospace Museum	F-15A	71-0286	

Location	Version	Serial	Notes	Location	Version	Serial	Notes
Military Aviation Museum Soesterberg, Holland	F-15A	74-0083	as '77-0132'	Eglin AFB Museum	F-15A	74-0124	
Evergreen Aviation Museum	F-15A	76-0014		National Warplane Museum, Elmira-Corning (NY)	F-15A	75-0026	
Lackland AFB	F-15A	71-0280	as '85-114'	Holloman AFB	F-15A	76-0037	
Wright Patterson AFB	F-15A	72-0119 and 76-0027		Otis ANGB	F-15	76-0040	
Luke AFB	F-15A	73-0085 and 73-0108		USAF Academy, Colorado Springs	F-15	76-0042	
Elmendorf AFB, Alaska	F-15A	74-0081		McCord AFB	F-15	76-0048	
Tyndall AFB	F-15A	74-0095		Lambert/ St Louis Airport	F-15	76-0088	
Sinsheim Museum, Denmark	F-15A	74-0109		Rickenbacker ANGB	F-15	77-0068	
Pima County Museum	F-15A	74-0118					

Appendix 5: Model Kits and Further Reading

The following list is limited only to those publications still in print at time of writing (December 2001).

McDonnell Douglas F-15A/B/C/D/E Eagle/Strike Eagle – Datagraph 6
by Dennis R. Jenkins
Published by Aerofax, August 1998 ISBN: 1857800818

McDonnell Douglas F-15 Eagle (Warbird Tech, Vol 9)
By Dennis R. Jenkins
Paperback, 100 pages (May 1997), Voyageur Press; ISBN: 0933424728

McDonnell-Douglas F-15 Eagle: A Photo Chronicle (Schiffer Military/Aviation History) by Bill

Holder and Mike Wallace
Paperback (October 1994), Schiffer Publishing,
Ltd; ISBN: 0887406629

*Lock-On No. 22: McDonnell Douglas F-15E Strike
Eagle*
By Francois Verlinden
Paperback, 36 pages (January 1, 1993), Verlinden
Productions, Inc.; ISBN: 1930607199

Lock-On No. 4: F-15C/D Eagle
by Francois Verlinden
36 pages (June 1, 1989), Verlinden Productions,
Inc.; ISBN: 9070932121

*Colors & Markings of the F-15 Eagle in Detail &
Scale, Part 1: Regular Air Force Fighter Wings*
(Colors & Markings, Vol 20)
ASIN: 0890241813

F-15 Eagle
By Peter Foster
Paperback, 64 pages (April 1998), Ian Allan Pub;
ISBN: 1882663225

Model kits

A range of F-15 model kits, super detailing sets,
decals and modellers reference books exists.

Tamiya and Hasegawa offer the most impressive
'out of the box' kits in 1:72, 1:48 and 1:32 scales.
Tamiya makes a 1:32 kit of F-15C 85-0125, the jet
in which Jon Kelk scored the first kill of *Desert
Storm*, as well as an F-15J and F-15E. As one
would expect of Tamiya, the kits are accurately
scaled, offer a range of panels and access hatches
which can be opened, and are extremely well
moulded. The same is true of Hasegawa, whose
range of 1:48 scale F-15 kits extends to a plethora
of versions and units – sixteen different kits in
total.

Verlinden is well known for its resin super-
detailing kits for the Hasegawa range, and the
author can vouch for the accuracy and quality of
these (VL0447 is for the F-15C and VL1648 for
the F-15E).

Most of the model kits mentioned above
feature good mouldings of the F-15 airframe, but
lack detail and accuracy in the cockpit. The
ACES II ejection seats in the Tamiya 1:32 scale
kits are especially short on detail, and require

either replacement or a little scratch building to
make them a little more authentic. Once again,
there is a range of manufacturers from which
super-detailing kits can be purchased.

For those wishing to keep costs down,
Revell/Monogram produces 1:32, 1:48 and 1:72
F-15 kits at a significantly reduced price, as do
Airfix and Academy. For those who wish to
scratch build, these kits offer value for money,
although the quality of the decals and the
moulding detail are understandably below that
of the Hasegawa and Tamyia kits. Eduard has a
comprehensive range of etched parts for the
larger scale F-15 kits.

A plethora of aftermarket decals in all scales is
available. Astra produces a good selection of
markings for European-based F-15s. Cutting
Edge has some good IDF/AF markings, and
Experts Choice offers markings for very early
Eagle squadrons. Superscale and Skys Decals
also offer a comprehensive range of decals across
the board, with the former having by far the
most extensive and interesting range of serial
numbers to chose from.

Xtracolor produces a range of excellent enamel
paints, including one especially for the F-15 –
Interior Blue/Grey (Xtracolor X159). This is an
excellent rendition of the colour found in the
avionics bays of F-15 variants, although
modellers are advised to study carefully where it
is used in the real thing before applying it
liberally over their models – some areas (such as
inside the F-15 radome) are not painted, or are
finished in a different colour (such as the inner
workings of the air-refuelling receptacle).

F-15 FS paint numbers are as follows:
F-15 71-0280 through to 73-0114 were painted
FS 35450 on top, FS 15450 beneath.
Pre-1990 F-15 deliveries were painted in FS 36320
and FS 36375.
The 'Mod Eagle' grey scheme introduced
thereafter saw these colours superseded by
FS 36251 and FS 36176.
The Strike Eagle in USAF service is painted in
Gunship Gray – FS 36114.
Saudi F-15s use the older FS 36320/FS 36375
scheme, with the exception of the 'S' model,
which uses the Mod Eagle scheme (albeit a
slightly varied version).

Index

Page numbers in *italics* refer to illustrations